ETHICAL LEADERSHIP
in Schools

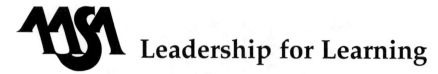

Leadership for Learning

Series Editors
Willis D. Hawley and E. Joseph Schneider

Joseph Murphy
Leadership for Literacy: Research-Based Practice, PreK–3

P. Karen Murphy, Patricia A. Alexander
Understanding How Students Learn: A Guide for Instructional Leaders

E. Joseph Schneider, Lara L. Hollenczer
The Principal's Guide to Managing Communication

Kenneth A. Strike
Ethical Leadership in Schools: Creating Community in an Environment of Accountability

Please call our toll-free number (800-818-7243)
or visit our website (www.corwinpress.com)
to order individual titles or the entire series.

ETHICAL LEADERSHIP

in Schools

Creating

Community

in an

Environment

of

Accountability

KENNETH A. STRIKE

CORWIN PRESS
A SAGE Publications Company
Thousand Oaks, California

For information:

Corwin Press
A Sage Publications Company
2455 Teller Road
Thousand Oaks, California 91320
www.corwinpress.com

Sage Publications Ltd.
1 Oliver's Yard
55 City Road
London EC1Y 1SP
United Kingdom

Sage Publications India Pvt. Ltd.
B-42, Panchsheel Enclave
Post Box 4109
New Delhi 110 017 India

Printed in the United States of America

Library of Congress Cataloging-in-Publication Data

Strike, Kenneth A.
Ethical leadership in schools: Creating community in an environment of accountability/Kenneth A. Strike.
        p. cm.—(Leadership for learning)
Includes bibliographical references and index.
ISBN 1-4129-1350-0 (cloth)—ISBN 1-4129-1351—9 (pbk.)
     1. School principals—Professional ethics. 2. Educational leadership—Moral and ethical aspects. I. Title. II. Series.
LB2831.9.S77 2007
371.2′012—dc22   2006007147

This book is printed on acid-free paper.

06   07   08   09   10   10 9 8 7 6 5 4 3 2 1

Acquisitions Editor:	Rachel Livsey
Editorial Assistant:	Phyllis Cappello
Production Editor:	Beth A. Bernstein
Copy Editor:	Kristin Fischer
Typesetter:	C&M Digitals (P) Ltd.
Proofreader:	Libby Larson
Indexer:	Judy Hunt
Cover Designer:	Rose Storey

Contents

Series Foreword

K enneth Strike has written an important book that will surely become a prized text in every school leader's bookcase. His book, *Ethical Leadership in Schools: Creating Community in an Environment of Accountability,* will be read initially with interest by administrators struggling with the ambiguities of their leadership role. But, as important, the book will be sought out again and again by school leaders who need to remind themselves about why they entered the profession and what it takes to remain true to the premise that "it's all about the children."

This book does not provide simple guidelines that define ethical leadership. The life of a school leader is filled with ethical dilemmas for which there are seldom easy answers.

Strike's book is about the fundamental question, How shall we live well together? Because schools should be good educational communities of students, parents, families, and supporters, Strike argues that ethics are all about creating and sustaining that reality.

What makes this book so fascinating as a good read and a helpful reference is Strike's willingness to delve into the dilemmas that challenge every school leader. A particular challenge, of course, is the need for school leaders to be accountable for providing a good education to all children. But members of a school's community may well have differing views about what constitutes acceptable accountability.

For example, many schools do an excellent job of educating the majority of their students. When this is the case, most parents and faculty members alike take pride in the school. And they are likely to resist any initiatives that threaten their perception of quality if this means reallocating resources or personnel to serve those students who may not be achieving as well as the majority. A school leader who suggests to faculty and parents that the school is going to begin to implement inclusive cooperative learning or special programs for students who have fallen behind can expect push back from parents of more academically talented children and their teachers.

Strike recognizes that school leaders are going to face constant challenges in their efforts to maximize their limited resources to provide maximum benefit to all students. Without question, it is extremely difficult to decide what produces the greatest good for the greatest number. An argument can be made—and undoubtedly will be made by some members of the school community—that resources ought to be invested where they can make the greatest impact. But such an argument leads some to conclude that the investment in disabled students or those performing way below their peers is hard to justify. A strong school leader may well argue that the school should be less concerned with an emphasis on programs that produce the greatest overall benefit and concentrate instead on investing in programs that help the students with the greatest need. Strike examines how leaders might make ethically grounded decisions about how to resolve such dilemmas and, in turn, justify their decisions to stakeholders.

In his book, Strike discusses the several ethical dilemmas the typical school administrator is likely to confront and offers reasonable, ethical ways of coming to grips with them. School leaders will be required to make judgments about what is desirable and at the same time possible for all their students, regardless of their different needs. Resources must be allocated fairly and appropriately to help all students achieve. Strike calls this leading from the principle of equal respect, that is, the duty to respect all people is not dependent on their particular capacities and their potential. Returning to his theme, Strike argues that our communities are stronger and better when all are cared for.

But how do principals sell this belief to their stakeholders? Strike answers this question over and over in his book, providing school leaders with a rationale for doing the right thing and methods for convincing others to act accordingly. It's likely that the school leaders will revisit Strike's book frequently as they construct arguments to convince their stakeholders to pursue actions that reflect a commitment to justice, fairness, and respect, and the desirability of inclusive communities rather than their private ends.

An ethical school leader, argues Strike, projects a clear image of the kind of community he wishes the school to be and then understands the notion of legitimate authority and legitimate decision making. Faculty members and parents, to select two primary groups within the stakeholder community, frequently will argue for their legitimate authority when challenging the principal's beliefs. And they will argue that if the principal is a democratic leader, he will do what they wish. Terms such as *democracy*, *professionalism*, *collegiality*, and *parents' rights* will be used to challenge the principal. In his book, Strike helps the principal understand that the notion of democratic leadership gives members of the school community a voice but doesn't confer upon them authority. That resides with the school leader. But that also means the principal needs to understand what it is to be a mindful conduit of legislative authority and what it takes to educate his stakeholders to the legitimacy of his role.

Kenneth Strike's book is one in a series being edited as part of the Leadership for Learning initiative of the American Association of School Administrators (AASA). The series attempts to enhance the capacity of school leaders to improve the quality of teaching so that all students learn at high levels. *Ethical Leadership in Schools: Creating Community in an Environment of Accountability* is a major addition to this series.

—*E. Joseph Schneider*

Series Introduction

The American Association of School Administrators (AASA) is the largest association in the world representing school system leaders and, in particular, school district superintendents. These educational leaders know that the quality of America's schools depends heavily on the ability of school principals. AASA recognizes that a pressing need exists to improve the skills and knowledge of current and prospective school leaders. To help address this need, AASA has put in place the Leadership for Learning initiative. This series of books plays a central role in this initiative.

The Leadership for Learning books address a broad range of knowledge and skills that school superintendents, exceptional principals, and researchers believe are essential to ensure effective leadership at the school level. The content of this series of books reflects the "leaders' standards" developed for state licensure by the Interstate School Leaders Licensure Consortium (ISLLC), which was composed of representatives from several professional organizations representing educators, policymakers, and scholars. These standards have been adopted by more than two thirds of the states as the criteria by which the qualifications of school principals should be judged. Although the books in the series can be thought of as parts of a coherent curriculum, individual books stand on their own as syntheses of relevant research and expert consensus about best practice. The series as a whole reflects the following commitments:

- All students should have the opportunity to maximize their potential for intellectual and social development.
- Enhancing the quality of teaching is the most important way to influence students' opportunities to learn.
- The actions of administrators, teachers, and school staff should be based on collaborative problem-solving focused on the systematic analysis of student performance and evidence of effective practice.
- School leaders need to foster the active engagement of parents and community organizations in the direct facilitation of student learning.

Leadership for Literacy examines the foundations of highly effective literacy programs in the primary grades. The focus is on the ways research on effective classrooms and productive schools can be used to ratchet up literacy achievement for all youth, especially children who have not fared well in school. The book helps leaders learn how to promote quality instruction, deepen the curriculum, and coordinate regular and special programs. The book also helps principals to promote higher reading achievement by fostering learning communities with schools and by nurturing collaboration between home and school.

—*Willis D. Hawley and E. Joseph Schneider,*
Series Editors

Preface

WHAT THIS BOOK IS ABOUT
AND WHY YOU SHOULD CARE

What is ethics about? What relevance does it have for school leaders? A common answer to the first question is that ethics is about *morality*: what is right and what is wrong. And certainly ethics is, in part, about what is right and what is wrong. This view of ethics, however, is too narrow, and, if you hold it, it will diminish the importance of understanding ethics for the practice of leadership.

Why is this view too narrow? Ethics, as I shall understand it here, concerns a larger question: How shall we live well together? Putting the central question of ethics this way focuses ethics on the nature of good communities. Schools should be good educational communities, and, for school leaders, the study of ethics should emphasize what makes a school a good educational community. Community is the essential relevance of ethics to leadership.

This larger question involves two main subquestions: What are the fundamental aims of good communities? and What is the nature of a fair basis of cooperation in good communities? When we ask these questions about schools, we want to know, first, what are their central aims, and, second, how these aims may be justly pursued. These questions, as we shall see, take us into a wide range of inquiries. We shall need to consider among other things the nature of the basic purposes of education in liberal democratic societies, the nature of intellectual and religious liberty, equality of educational opportunity, democracy and legitimate authority, and fair decision making.

To focus a book on the ethics of leadership *merely* on morality, on the question of what is right and what is wrong, tends to overemphasize personal conduct and disconnects ethics from the art of good leadership. If we are merely concerned with what is right and wrong, we may decide that leaders should be truthful, not steal from their schools, not be racist or sexist, avoid conflicts of interest, and make fair decisions. And certainly leaders should do these things. But when we had observed these things, we would not know very much about schools or good leadership. These norms are rules of conduct in any institution or community, but they are also disconnected from educational purposes and the nature of good education. The larger view I shall take of ethics is intended to reconnect ethics with the nature of good education, good educational communities, and good leadership.

This book also concerns accountability. While it is not entirely about accountability, it turns to a discussion of accountability frequently, and this helps to tie the various inquiries in the book together. And there is a persistent theme about accountability argued in this book: To be responsibly accountable, educators need to have a coherent vision of the education they wish to provide and how they ought to provide it.

Leaders should use such data about their school's performance that various accountability schemes may provide to make judgments about whether they are providing a good education, but they should not allow the various performance measures employed in these schemes to define a good education. Test scores should be one measure of educational effectiveness but not its meaning. When we allow our measures of a good education to become its meaning, we run the risk of various vices of accountability, such as gaming and goals displacement. We can avoid these vices by creating schools that are strong, ethical communities with a coherent vision of their mission.

THE PLAN OF THIS BOOK

In Chapter 1, I develop the idea that ethics is concerned with good communities and lay out some of the other themes of this book. Following this introductory chapter, in Chapters 2 and 3, I discuss some of the basic goals of education and the idea of intellectual community. The themes here are simple: The central goals of education all involve cognitive development. This, in turn, requires that schools be intellectual communities where ideas and their debate and discussion are valued.

In the central part of the book, Chapters 4 and 5 (but including Chapter 3 as well), I discuss what I call *constitutional essentials*: intellectual liberty, freedom of religion, equality, and democracy. Here the focus is on the central norms of liberal democracies. How shall we understand these norms of fair social cooperation in an educationally relevant way?

Chapter 5, which considers legitimate authority in relation to accountability, also provides a transition into the final section of the book, where we discuss ethical decision making in Chapter 6 and accountability in Chapter 7. An account of the ethics of accountability is central in these chapters.

At the end of the introductory chapter, I have provided the reader with a more detailed sketch of each chapter and its contents.

THEMES AND THREADS

Are there threads that tie these chapters together? There are several. Let me mention three. First, the fact that we live in and aspire to be a liberal democratic society is central to this work. Among the norms that should shape our schools are those of liberty, equality, and democratic community. I refer to these as *constitutional essentials*. They are among the central principles of fair cooperation in our society.

The second unifying theme is the *ethics of accountability*. For good or ill, accountability is a reality of the lives of school leaders. I do not address accountability as a policy matter. While I have many views on this, I try to keep them out of this book. School leaders (especially those being newly minted) are not asked to make policy. They are asked to comply with it. Yet educational policy interacts with the culture and the norms of schools. Often whether policy succeeds or fails depends on that interaction. My purpose in this book is not to praise or condemn accountability, it is to discuss with you how to respond to it responsibly.

The final unifying theme is that *community counts*. The fundamental task of the school leader is to create communities that are competent, caring, collegial, and, of course, educative. That is not an easy task because there are many factors that tend to pull communities apart. It is, however, essential to good education, ethical schools, and responsible accountability.

WHY YOU SHOULD CARE

Why should you care about ethics? One answer to this question is that, if you are to address the complex issues that you will face, you need answers to the kinds of questions I address. You need a view of what counts as a good education and of the importance and role of constitutional ideals such as liberty and equality. You need a coherent view of your own role and your own authority and of how to deal with conflicting demands made on you. You need a view of the norms of ethical decision making. Finally, you need a view of the ethics of accountability. In short, you need a moral compass to guide you through a jungle of complex and conflicting demands.

A second answer is that you need a view of what constitutes a healthy and effective educational community. As you are not yet education tsar (and I trust you do not aspire to this), the relevance of the answers you achieve to the questions I pose is not so much that you can proceed to act unilaterally on them as it is that you can create an educational community in which answers to these questions are sought and reflected upon. Creating healthy and effective deliberative communities is the very center of your job.

What should you expect to obtain from this book? I will occasionally offer some concrete advice. But I am less interested in generating specific guidelines than I am in helping you to think through some of the ethical complexities that are likely to occur in your professional practice and to generate a reflective stance on the issues involved. Perspective and reflection may require developing some complex concepts or even creating a language for discussing them. Concrete advice often additionally requires detailed knowledge of a context, and contexts vary. Hence, detailed advice and precise recommendations may not travel well. Thus, this book aims to provide perspective, shape aspirations, and enable understanding more than it aims at concrete recommendations and recipes. I hope to put you in a place to provide your own ethical advice.

Corwin Press gratefully acknowledges the contributions of the following reviewers:

John C. Hughes
Principal
Public School 48
The Joseph R. Drake School
Bronx, NY

Susan N. Imamura
Principal
Manoa Elementary School
Honolulu, HI

Ira Pernick
High School Principal
Robert Kennedy Community High School
Flushing, NY

Patricia B. Schwartz
Principal
Thomas Jefferson Middle School
Teaneck, NJ

Paul Young
Executive Director
Retired Principal
West Elementary School
Lancaster, OH

About the Author

**Kenneth A. Strike** is a professor of cultural foundations of education and of philosophy at Syracuse University. He is also professor emeritus at Cornell University, where he taught from 1971 to 2000, and is former chair of the Department of Education Policy Studies at the University of Maryland. He earned his BA from Wheaton College and his MA and PhD from Northwestern University. He has been a Distinguished Visiting Professor at the University of Alberta. He is a past president of the Philosophy of Education Society and was elected to the National Academy of Education in 1993. He was a member of the National Research Council Committee on School Finance, Equity, Adequacy, and Productivity from 1996 to 1999.

His principal interests are professional ethics and political philosophy as they apply to matters of educational practice and policy. He is the author of a number of books and well more than a hundred articles. Recent books include *The Ethics of Teaching*, *The Ethics of School Administration*, *Liberal Justice, and the Marxist Critique of Schooling*, and *Ethics and College Student Life*. Papers of note include "Professionalism, Democracy, and Discursive Communities: Normative Reflections on Restructuring" in the *American Education Research Journal*, "The Moral Role of Schooling in a Liberal Democratic Society" in the *Review of Research in Education*, "The Moral Responsibilities of Educators" in *Handbook of Research on Teacher Education*, "Can Schools Be Communities: The Tension Between Shared Values and Inclusion" in *Educational Administration Quarterly*, "Freedom of Conscience and Illiberal Socialization: The Congruence Argument" in the *Journal of Philosophy of Education*, "On the Construction of Public Speech: Pluralism and Public Reason" in *Educational Theory*, and "Centralized Goal Formation, Citizenship, and Educational Pluralism: Accountability in Liberal Democracies" in *Educational Policy*.

Professor Strike delivered the 1999 Kohlberg Memorial Lecture at the annual meeting of the Association for Moral Education. The address was published as "Liberalism, Communitarianism, and the Space Between: In

Praise of Kindness" in the *Journal of Moral Education*, and he gave the keynote address at the Great Britain Philosophy of Education Society in 2000. This address was published as "Schools as Communities: Four Metaphors, Three Models, and a Dilemma or Two" in the *Journal of Philosophy of Education*. He has written on a variety of other topics, including school reform, desegregation, affirmative action, and religious liberty in education. His current work concerns the exploration of the normative aspects of school reform, emphasizing the notion of schools as communities. He is the recipient of a grant from the Spencer Foundation for this work.

Professor Strike lives in Thendara, New York, a small village in the Adirondack Mountains, in a house on the shore of the Moose River on which he regularly canoes, kayaks, and only occasionally bothers the fish.

Moral Principles and Moral Principals?

An Introduction

A SCENARIO

The scenario that follows is the dominant example in this book. I will discuss some of its features in this introductory chapter and will return to it a number of times in the book, altering it as though it were about different levels of education: elementary, middle, or high school.

Imagine that you are the principal of a school in a large district. Your school, like your district, has a diverse population. It does not have the extreme poverty that characterizes a few of the schools in your district, yet your community is not wealthy. Students for the most part come from middle- and working-class families who own modest homes. The percentage of children on free and reduced lunch is lower than the district average.

Your school is successful in a district where many schools are not. You have worked hard to make your school into a learning community. Your teachers work well together. Parents and community members are included in some of the deliberations and feel they are valued partners in the school.

Under your leadership, your teachers have developed a curriculum and instructional strategies that you and they believe to be first-rate. While basic skills are not neglected, the program is designed to teach advanced cognitive skills and to develop creativity. Teachers cooperate in its implementation and meet frequently to discuss problems.

Your teachers did a great deal of background research on this curriculum, and they believe that the curriculum and their instructional strategies are supported by a significant body of educational research. Its merits have been confirmed through their own experience, and they have modified the program where needed. Parents understand the program, were regularly consulted while it was being developed, and support it.

Your state has a series of tests that the students in your school must take. Results are reported in the local papers, and there is much pressure on schools to do well. This has not been a problem for you. Your students do well. Moreover, while the program your teachers developed under your leadership was not designed to be aligned with these tests, it seems more than adequate to prepare your students to succeed on them. While some parents have complained about the amount of time their children spend taking tests, many teachers and parents have felt that the fact that their children score well on these tests is a validation of their efforts. They are happy to be accountable.

Moreover, the data from the tests have been helpful in the continuing assessment of and reflection on the program. Among other things, test results have helped make it clear that while your students perform well on average, it is not the case that all students do well. It has been of particular concern to you that those students who are on free and reduced lunch are overrepresented in the group of students who are performing poorly.

Other schools in your district have not done well, even on average. Your district is one of the more poorly performing ones in your state. That its central office, superintendent, and board of education have had a history of conflict and turnover has not helped it focus on the problem of educating its large number of poor and minority students.

After much soul-searching and a fair amount of squabbling, your district has produced a plan to deal with this matter. Among the provisions of the plan are three that will directly impact your school. First, the district has insisted that the curriculum in each of its schools be tightly aligned with state tests. This will require considerable revision of your current curriculum. Second, the district has mandated that review of released or sample test items be incorporated into instruction on a regular basis in all subjects for which there are tests. Finally, the district has required that whenever a test is to be given, during the two weeks prior to testing, significant instructional time is to be devoted to test preparation and taking practice tests.

The district justified these requirements by claiming that it believed that the state's tests were good tests aligned with state standards; hence, educational practices that focused on them served to focus the attention of the district's schools on teaching what they should be teaching and, if this amounted to "teaching to the test," to do so was nothing more than to emphasize essential content.

The teachers and parents at your school were most unhappy. They did not wish to alter their current curriculum and instructional practices, and since their students were doing quite well, they saw no reason why they should. They did not agree that they were merely being asked to teach sound subject matter in ways that had proven successful. They claimed that they were being required to focus on rote memorization of facts rather than on higher cognitive skills and creativity, and they quickly (if not very originally) dubbed the pedagogy they were expected to employ "drill and kill." Meetings were called, and contentious letters were written. (We will read portions of these letters in Chapter 5.) There was criticism not only of the wisdom of the board's new policies but also of how they were achieved. A number of people argued that the board members were playing politics by attempting to divert attention from some of their own failings. They were more concerned with sound bites than sound education.

Eventually, demands were made of you. You were asked to return to the board of education and secure an exemption for your school from these requirements. Failing this, you were asked to lead an effort to work around these board mandates and, it was privately suggested by a few, to subvert them. Several interesting suggestions were made about the nature of "creative program characterizations" that might be made to the central office on various reports that had to be filed. A little imaginative reporting might secure the required autonomy needed by your school, and no one was likely to look too closely at the program of a successful school.

You were not pleased with these suggestions. You worked for the board of education. So did the teachers. While you understood the concerns of the parents and teachers about the changes, you also thought that they had over-reacted and that the board's strategy might benefit instruction in the district. Indeed, you wondered if it might not benefit some of your students. After all, not all of your students succeeded, and you were concerned that too many poor students were left behind. The teachers and parents of your school, you worried, were a bit too satisfied with their program and had not adequately come to terms with the fact that it did not work for everyone. You were also reluctant to misrepresent your school's program to the board, even for a good and just cause. No one had used the unpleasant term lie *when they suggested how you were to represent your school to the board, but it felt like lying to you.*

PROLOGUE

In this chapter I will use the preceding scenario to introduce some issues about the ethics of leadership. I will also explain my vision of what ethics is about. Ethics concerns the fundamental question, How shall we live well together?

Ethics has often been understood to involve two basic questions: What is good? and What is right? The question on how to live well together focuses discussion of these two questions on the nature of good communities. "What is good?" concerns the fundamental aims of communities. "What is right?" concerns the principles and shared understandings that enable social cooperation. Good communities have worthy aims and a fair basis of cooperation. I will encourage you to view ethical leadership as the art of creating good school communities.

ETHICS AND LEADERSHIP

A number of ethical issues are embedded in the scenario with which this chapter began. I would suppose that most readers will have recognized the suggestion that you "creatively" characterize your program to the board of education as an ethical issue. May you lie for a good cause? Can you be deceptive even if you don't actually assert something that is false?

Other candidates for ethical issues emerge from the suggestion that, while on average the students in your school are doing well, some are not. These students are disproportionately poor. Are there issues about equality here? There are several. One is equality of educational opportunity. What does it mean? What does it require? If some students are not doing as well as others, does it inevitably follow that they have been treated unequally? How would we decide this? What should we do about it?

A related issue is the ethics of resource distribution. You are worried that some of the less affluent students in your school are not doing well. Suppose you propose that to help these students catch up, you will provide them with additional resources. Is that ethical when this decision lessens the resources available to others? How would we decide this? What constitutes a just distribution of educational resources?

A third issue of equality concerns the nature of a community in which all are equal even though they are also different in many respects. What kind of community is this? How do its members relate to one another? How do we respect diversity and still promote a democratic culture? What is a fair basis of cooperation in a community in which there is much difference?

The scenario also raises a number of questions of legitimate authority. The parents and teachers in your school have raised questions about the board of education's decision by challenging the *merits* of the decision. They think it to be unwise. But they have also raised issues about the *legitimacy* of the board's decision. They have hinted that the decision was intended to serve the needs of the members of the board rather than of the children in its schools. If this is true, does it make the decision illegitimate? Need illegitimate decisions be obeyed?

They might have pressed the matter further. Why is the board allowed to decide these matters? The parents of your school's children might argue that they should have the final say about how their children are educated. After all, these students are their children. They do not belong to the board of education.

Your teachers, in turn, might argue that they should be entitled to the most authoritative say about how the children under their care are educated. After all, they are the professionals, the ones with relevant experience, and the ones who work directly with the students and who best know what they need.

Both your parents and teachers might argue that the educational program at your school was achieved by a process of democratic deliberation and consultation involving parents and teachers, and it was the product of a consensus among these key actors. Why is a distant board of lay people who don't know the local situation, who don't know much about education, who may be using the board of education to further political careers, and whose interests are not significantly affected by how well these children perform permitted to override the considered judgment of those who know what is best for these children and of those who care most for them? Who elected them?

Of course the answer to the final question in most places is that the citizens of the school district did. Why do these citizens, who may not have children in your school and may know little about it, get to select those who decide what goes on in your school?

In these few sentences, we have begun to articulate a tension between two conceptions of democracy. One conception sees democracy as a process of local deliberation that seeks a reasoned consensus about what is good and fair for the community to do. When school leaders are asked to be democratic leaders, this is often the kind of democracy people have in mind. But another conception sees democracy as concerned with elections and representation. Sovereignty does not rest with the local community. It rests with an elected legislature. How do these conceptions fit together? Do they fit together?

Several different principles of legitimation are appealed to in these comments: decisions should be made by those who are elected by the citizenry to do so, decisions should be made by those most directly affected, decisions should be made by those most competent to make them, and decisions should be made via the deliberations of the local community. There is something to be said for all of these views. How are they to be balanced? When they conflict, which is to be preferred?

A closely related issue is the ethics of decision making. Ethical decisions must be legitimate decisions. Hence, to know when a decision is ethical, we must have a view of who is entitled to make it, that is, who has legitimate authority. But ethical decisions have other features: they aim at worthy ends, they treat people fairly and respect their rights, they respect evidence and argument, and they are transparent and open to debate.

Worthy ends? How do we know if our ends are worthy? Consider how this question arises from our scenario. Some of your parents and teachers have dubbed the board's mandates with the pejorative label "drill and kill." What does that mean, and why might one think that it is objectionable?

Very likely the phrase is meant to imply that *drill* is tedious and *kills* the interest in learning. Is this right? Perhaps, but something more is at stake. Educators often object to drills because they believe that the kind of learning that is of most worth aims at understanding and creativity and involves reflection, argument, and the appraisal of evidence. The teachers and parents of your school seem to believe this. Drills do not seem to involve reflection or aim at understanding or reasoned conclusions. This suggests that underlying the view that education should involve understanding and the assessment of evidence may be an ideal of character concerning what we want our students to become. We want them to be able to decide for themselves on the basis of adequate evidence. We want them to become autonomous, self-governing people.

There may also be an ideal of citizenship and democratic community involved. We wish for our society to be a certain form of political community, a democracy. Arguably, a democracy requires citizens who are able to engage one another in dialogue and to discover and support policies that are reasonable and sustain the common good.

If concerns such as these motivate the objections of parents and teachers to drill and kill, then they have raised some serious objections to board policy. While these objections may be mistaken, they appeal to values that are profound and deeply held. Their objections are not just about the nature of effective pedagogy or what is required to raise test scores. If these objections have merit, then the board is mandating a kind of education that rubs up against some of the deepest moral and ethical convictions of liberal democratic societies. Perhaps they have a mistaken view about how to educate children so that they (and we) can live well together in a democratic society. If these objections are wrong, then it is important to understand why.

ETHICS AND MORALITY: WHAT ARE THEY? WHAT IS ETHICS ABOUT?

Let's consider the types of issues that we have raised. There are issues of personal conduct: Is it ever right to lie? There are issues concerning the aims of education: Should our schools aim at producing autonomous individuals? Should they aim at producing good citizens? And what do these aims mean and require? There are issues of rights: Do students have a right not to be indoctrinated? Do they have a right to equal opportunity? There are issues of legitimate authority: What is the basis of the school board's authority? What is the basis of your authority? Who is entitled to a say about educational matters? To whom may we be made accountable for our actions? There are issues that concern community norms: What does it mean to be a democratic community? What does it mean to be an intellectual or an educational community?

Why are such issues ethical issues? Historically, ethics has been viewed as an inquiry into the nature of good living. It addresses the broad question, How shall we live? or, as I prefer, How shall we live well together?

Earlier I suggested that this broad question can be divided into two further questions, those concerned with what is *good* and those concerned with what is *right*. Each of these questions poses others.

Questions concerned with what is good are: What ends are worth pursuing? What activities are worth doing? What kinds of lives are worth living? What is the nature of human flourishing? What kinds of people must we become if we are to live well? How can we educate so as to produce people of this sort? What kinds of communities and societies do we need if people are to be able to lead good lives? and How can we create people who are able to sustain and function in these communities? These questions start with a concern for the nature of those goods and activities that are intrinsically worthwhile or worthwhile for their own sake. Every view of education presupposes answers to such questions.

Questions about what is right involve many issues about personal conduct: May I lie? May I steal? and May I kill? But there are other questions: What is the nature of legitimate authority? When must I obey the commands of another, and when must others obey me? What rights do I have? What duties and responsibilities do I have? How are social resources justly distributed? and How are decisions fairly made? Such "ought" questions concern the rules and principles that govern the interaction of members of the community and that assign to them various rights and responsibilities. They establish a fair basis for social cooperation.

To understand what makes a community (including a school community) a good one, we must answer both of these broad questions. That is, we must know something about the fundamental goods at which the community aims and the moral principles that govern interaction in the community. Communities are associations in which individuals cooperate to realize shared aims. Good communities pursue worthy aims, and, if they are to function well, they must have a shared conception of the rules and principles that govern the cooperation of their members in the pursuit of these aims.

Thus, to answer questions about the ends at which a community aims and the principles that govern the interactions of its members is not just to address the question, How shall we live? Instead, it is to address the question, How shall we live well together? Ethics, ultimately, is about the shape of human communities in which people can flourish and about the basis for social cooperation in such communities.

ETHICS AND PLURALISM

One concern about this view of ethics is that it is potentially oppressive. Perhaps when we have discovered answers to questions about the good communities, we will have developed a view that assumes there is one kind of life that is good for all and that all must cooperate to achieve it. This is the path that leads to total community, oppression, and the inquisition. It is not a path we should take.

While human communities do exist to further cooperation in pursuit of shared ends, it does not follow that all ends must be shared. While human communities must have agreements about how decisions are to be made, it does not follow that communities may make all decisions on behalf of their members. Good communities may be united in the pursuit of some aims and quite diverse in other respects. The task for educators is often to discover how to pursue shared aims while encouraging appropriate diversity. How shall we approach this task?

Here is one way to think about the issues of unity and diversity: Our society is liberal and democratic. Liberal societies emphasize individual rights and freedom. Democratic societies emphasize collective decision-making and the pursuit of common goods. Liberal democratic societies are often characterized by the tension between democratic decision making and individual freedom.

The freedoms that liberal societies grant their members impose restraints on the scope of democratic decision making, permit members of the society to choose their own ends, and enable their free participation in democratic decision making. There is a familiar list of such freedoms, including freedom of speech, press, and association; freedom of religion; and a right to privacy and property. To say that people have such rights is to say (among other things) that legislatures may not pass laws that restrict them. The First Amendment to the U.S. Constitution begins, "Congress shall make no law . . ."

Thus, liberal societies have an answer to the claim that ethical inquiry leads to oppressive communities dominated by an imposed conception of the good. It is that people have rights—rights that impose limits on what the community may decide and that require the community to treat them freely and equally. Part of our inquiry must concern the nature of these rights and how they constrain and shape educational communities.

Now we must address a second concern. Sometimes individual rights are viewed as though they were anticommunal in their character. Liberal societies are often described as being individualistic, and this characterization is often meant as an accusation.

This accusation seems to me to be wrong. These rights do restrain the scope of democratic decision making, but they shape community as much as they restrain it. These rights tell us what we believe to be a fair basis for social cooperation. They tell us that the political community we want must be one in which the basis of cooperation is not, for example, a shared religion or some other shared orthodoxy. It is one in which people are free and equal. It is one in which people may freely participate in collective decision making. The political community of liberal democracy is thus limited, but the aim is not to produce a society in which people act solely as individuals in the pursuit of their own ends; its aim is to produce a political community in which people may flourish in diverse ways while cooperating fairly in pursuing common goods.

One conclusion of this view is that in liberal democratic societies, the government may not require orthodoxy of belief or of faith as the basis of political community; nor, since they are agents of government, may public schools. It follows that the aims of the schools of liberal democratic societies must not assume such orthodoxies.

Yet there must be some goods at which the schools of a liberal democratic society can aim without oppressing some of their members. If there were not, we could not (or should not) have common schools. What are these goods? The answer to this question awaits in the next chapter. Here let me note only that the aims of public schools must be big-tented, that is, they must be of such a nature as to guide the education of children from diverse cultures and faiths while allowing all to be equal citizens. The aims of common schools must be inclusive aims.

I will also argue that the aims of public education should not be merely instrumental. One way to try to make public schools big-tented is to disavow any interest in considering the nature of good lives. We merely provide basic skills and essential knowledge, believing that such skills and knowledge can be useful to all, regardless of the kind of lives they seek to lead. We aim at universal instrumentalities.

This, I believe, is not a good response. Of course, we must provide basic skills and knowledge. But we must also help our students become good citizens and have worthy conceptions of how they will live their lives and what they will live them for. To do otherwise, I will argue, is corrosive of educational community and the solidarity on which democratic societies depend. The idea, then, is not to lapse into instrumentalism but to promote a big-tented vision of a good education that is inclusive of diverse cultures, faiths, and aspirations.

Thus, the claim that people have rights that are sometimes against the authority of the community does not reject the idea that ethics concerns answering the question of how we shall live well together in favor of an individualistic society. Rather, it insists that we answer the question in a certain way. It insists that in our public institutions, the goods at which we aim are goods that can be the goods of all.

It also insists that goods that cannot be the aims of all be those of communities that are free associations. Such communities (e.g., places of worship) are important to the health of free societies, but they do not act with the endorsement and authority of the state. This is part of what we mean by pluralism in liberal democratic societies. We limit the scope of the political community so that a diversity of communities can flourish. That liberal democratic societies do not view all goods as public goods does not reject the idea that goods are sought in a community. It tells us something about the kinds of communities we want. It says that part of human flourishing is freedom.

ETHICS AND MORALITY

I have said that ethics addresses two central questions: What is good? and What is right? Sometimes the notion of morality is understood to be concerned with the second question. Morality, in this view, is the part of ethics that deals with questions of right and wrong, with rights and duties, but does not concern itself with what is good.

There is a tendency for modern discussions of ethics to emphasize morality and pay less attention to questions about what is good. Why? One reason might be that there is no way to decide what is good. What is good, many believe, is a matter of personal taste. Even if it is possible to know what is good, the decision about what is good is one to be made by individuals, not by the society. Individuals have a right to choose those goods that they will attempt to realize in their lives. Inquiry into what is good is therefore impossible and potentially oppressive. Perhaps ethics *should* be reduced to morality.

The consequence of a focus on morality is to emphasize the question of the nature of a fair basis of social cooperation and to claim that people are entitled to pursue a freely chosen conception of the good with those whom they choose to associate with. If we wish to be a free society, there is much to commend such a view.

However, the reduction of ethics to morality is a mistake, and a particularly problematic mistake for educators and school leaders. I would respond to the two problems with inquiry into the nature of the good as follows. First, it is possible to inquire into the nature of the good. (I will engage in such an inquiry in the next chapter.) It does not follow that the good must be the same for everyone. Indeed, I believe that one feature of good lives is that they are lived "from the inside." Nothing will be experienced as good if it is experienced as something imposed.

Moreover, what one experiences as good is affected by nature and culture. We are different in some ways from the outset. Our cultures further shape our wants and needs. When individual differences and enculturation have done their work, we will experience our good in different things. Every school leader should understand and respect this.

How, then, can we think productively about the good? There are two complementary approaches. One that I have just suggested is that we can look for those goods that are big-tented. Philosopher Martha Nussbaum (1990) coined a useful phrase for such goods: They should be *thick, but vague.* An example of such goods (which I shall discuss more fully in the next chapter) is that people tend to enjoy activities that develop their capacities and engage the capacities they have developed. More simply, people enjoy becoming good at something and doing what they have become good at.

This view of what makes something good has substance to it. It provides guidance about how to live well, and it provides guidance to educators about the goals of education. It says that we should help students discover worthwhile activities that they can master. At the same time, it is a view of the good that is big-tented because it is vague. It can be realized through a wide range of activities and expressed through various cultures. It does not oppress or exclude.

A second approach is to note that liberal democratic societies can themselves be viewed as good because they permit and encourage human flourishing in a variety of forms and because they are just. They enable a diversity of good lives and permit us to enjoy and learn from those who are different from us. Others become our resources. We become their resources. Moreover, being a member of such a society is a good in its own right. Being part of such a just society is itself part of living well. Our view of the aims of education may then be informed by the characteristics required of individuals if they are to be flourishing members of liberal democratic societies. We can, then, think about the good and do so in a way that informs our view of education.

ETHICS AND LEADERSHIP

This is a book about the *ethics* of leadership, not just its morality. When ethics collapses into morality, the tendency is to disconnect morality from the nature of good communities and their goals and ideals. Moral rules and principles become the generic rules and principles of any and all communities: Don't steal, don't lie, respect people's rights, and so forth. These are the morality of schools and school leaders because they are the morality of all institutions and associations.

I want to provide a view of ethics that is internal to the role of the educational leader. This means that I need to talk about the goals of education and how moral rules and principles contribute to the realization of these goals. I want schools in which children flourish and learn to flourish. The ethic of school leaders needs to be an ethic for educational institutions that teach children how to flourish in liberal democratic societies.

I have said that one very general way to characterize the role of leaders is that they must create healthy, functional, and good educational communities. To explain this I must talk about how ethics furthers healthy educational communities. I cannot do this with a generic conception of morality. It requires a view of educational communities that are informed by a conception of human flourishing and by how moral principles shape the interactions of the members of educational communities to realize their vision.

When we ask if it is okay to lie to benefit one's students, if students have a right to free speech, and what it means to treat people equally, we are seeking the basis of social cooperation in educational institutions. We should not be satisfied with generic answers to these questions. We should want to understand why truth-telling is important to good education. We should want to understand how the expression and consideration of dissenting views serves educational goals. We should want to understand how equal educational opportunity shapes people to be good citizens in democratic societies. Generic answers will not serve.

At worst, relying on a kind of generic morality to understand the ethics of leadership can contribute to an attitude toward morality that sees it as a kind of necessary evil or an inconvenience rather than as the basis for fair cooperation in educational institutions.

When we are thinking in this way, what we are really doing is viewing decision making in a certain way. We are saying to ourselves that first we decide what actions are most likely to efficiently serve chosen ends. Once we have chosen a course of action, we then ask ourselves if acting in this way violates any moral rules. The liability of thinking in this way is that we do not ask whether actions we have chosen are consistent with the norms that are appropriate to a community with worthy educational aims. Moreover, we are tempted to cut corners when morality seems inconvenient to the pursuit of worthy ends.

Consider due process. School leaders sometimes chafe at the necessity to follow various rules of due process when they evaluate teachers. They may experience these rules largely as constraints on their authority and judgment. I have heard more than one school leader complain, "I know this teacher is incompetent. Now I have to spend months or years proving it to the satisfaction of lawyers and courts. Time and treasure are wasted, and children are harmed." When we think something like this, compliance becomes legalistic and separated from the educational purposes of due process. And we are tempted to a kind of arrogance—one that says that so long as our hearts are pure and our intentions noble, we should not have to follow rules that prevent us from making those decisions we know to be good ones. We are tempted to cut corners so as to produce good outcomes.

But we can also think of the requirements of due process as serving values that are central and internal to good educational communities—fairness to those evaluated and rationality in decision making. A sense that one will be treated fairly is community building. It helps people bond with the institution, its purposes, and its work. Moreover, being fair models fairness to our students. It is part of an education for citizenship.

Also, the rules of due process can be viewed as a kind of institutionalized rationality—a specification of how to collect evidence, make reliable judgments based on it, and produce good decisions. In evaluation and other personnel matters, good decisions produce good teachers. Moreover, they also model a key educational good—the rule of reason in human affairs. Fairness and rationality are not just constraints on efficient action toward desired ends. They are part of establishing educative communities.

Or consider accountability. You might say that your responsibility is to raise those test scores, and that you will do so by the most efficient means that do not violate some moral principle. You will not lie or cheat, but you will employ the most efficient pedagogical means to improve scores. If drill and kill will do it, then drill and kill it is. That, after all, is what it means to be accountable: to adopt the most efficient means to achieve publicly agreed upon benchmarks of achievement.

In contrast, you might employ the test scores you achieve as one piece of evidence about how your students are doing in realizing an educational program that you and your school view as having merit because it (ulti-mately) serves a praiseworthy conception of human flourishing, and you might embark on an inquiry as to how you can improve test scores in edu-cationally productive ways. You can view test scores as a measure of whether you are providing a good education but not as specifying its mean-ing. Once you say this, you will need to develop a conception of a good education to provide a context for understanding the meaning of test scores.

To take the latter stance toward being accountable in a responsible way is to engage in an ethical inquiry that extends beyond mere morality. It must be informed by a vision of human flourishing. This is what the dis-cussion of the board of education's policy described in our scenario has begun. It is what complaints about drill and kill are ultimately about. Your school needs to explore what lies behind these clichés. While your teach-ers ultimately need to comply with the board of education's legitimate requirements, they need to do so in a way that serves a praiseworthy and articulate vision of a good education.

In this book, morality is viewed as only part of ethics. This is a book about the ethics of leadership, not about mere morality. Morality must inform us about how to create good educative communities.

LYING FOR GOOD ENDS

I am hopeful that your instinctive reaction to the suggestion that you mislead the school board so as to preserve the program of your school is to reject it out of hand. The appropriate ethical response to this suggestion is to do the best you can to make the case for your school's program and, if you do not succeed, to explain to the people in your school that it is now their obligation to respond as productively as possible to board policy. If this is your instinctive response, you may not feel the need of a justification for it.

Discussing it will be productive nonetheless. As a school leader, you will have many opportunities to engage in deceptive behavior—if not to the board of education, then to teachers, parents, or students. One of the most persistent temptations of leaders is to lie for what they perceive to be a good cause. A discussion of lying may help to put deception in perspec-tive. Even if you are altogether saintly about truth-telling, the discussion of lying that follows will be used to introduce some concepts that will be useful in considering ethical issues in other contexts.

With this in mind, consider some ways to addresses the issue. (The following discussion owes much to Bok [1999].)

THREE HISTORICAL APPROACHES

One approach to lying emphasizes the concept of equal respect for persons and appeals to an ideal like the golden rule. Is lying wrong? We decide this by noting that we do not want to be lied to. We would not, to paraphrase

Immanuel Kant (1956), be willing to make lying into a universal rule of human conduct. Moreover, when people lie to us, they treat us as instruments to their ends rather than as persons who are ends in their own right and deserving of respect. On this view, good ends do not justify unethical means. Someone who took this stance might claim, "Lying is simply wrong. Lying to the school board would not be justified even if it might produce good ends." The duty to respect persons means that people have a right not to be lied to, and we have a duty not to lie to them.

Another historical theory focuses its attention on the consequences of our actions. A classical formulation called utilitarianism (e.g., see Bentham & Mill, 1961; Smart & Williams, 1973) says that the best actions are those that produce the greatest good for the greatest number. This theory invites us to consider the range of consequences of an action, determine the desirability of these consequences, and make a judgment as to which set of likely outcomes is most desirable. Here one would object to lying because it generally has bad consequences. Note, however, that this seems to open the door a bit wider to lying when lying produces more good than harm. Indeed, utilitarianism might be construed to require lying under such circumstances.

A third approach, communitarianism (see MacIntyre, 1981), reminds us that we are members of a community. This community has purposes and traditions, as well as members. We owe a debt of loyalty to these purposes, traditions, and members. Lying, from this perspective, is wrong because it erodes trust, undermines the solidarity on which effective communities rely if they are to accomplish their purposes, and is inconsistent with the purposes of educational communities.

In this book, my approach is closest to communitarianism. However, I will not enter into a debate between these and other theories. Resolving such philosophical debates has only modest value so far as practical, ethical decision making is concerned. Moreover, I do not believe that there is such a thing as one right moral theory. Moral theories typically attempt to systematize and explain our moral experience and put it on a firm, rational basis. They may also illuminate it by showing us more clearly what is involved in our decisions. However, moral theories that claim there is one central moral good, such as respect, utility, or community, may also distort moral experience.

Hence, in this book, I will not often appeal to the kinds of systematic theories that philosophers have developed to discuss practical ethical problems. I will, however, sometimes call attention to ethical ideals that capture what these theories take to be central to ethical decision making. In what I have just stated, we can see three ideals at work: respect for persons, benefit maximization, and community. The first invites us to view others as ends in themselves and entitled to equal respect, the second to maximize good outcomes, and the third to create and sustain healthy communities. Bringing these ideals to bear on issues is quite central to ethical decision-making. We can illustrate these ideals by seeing how they apply to lying.

LYING AND EQUAL RESPECT

Consider some questions suggested by the ideal of equal respect. You might quite reasonably view being lied to as a sign that you are not respected. Those who lie to you treat you as a means to their ends. Reverse your role with someone on the board of education. Would you be willing to be lied to under these circumstances? As a school board member, you would have a public responsibility for the welfare of all the children in the schools of your district. You would be trying to make judgments about effective policies that are in the best interest of all. You would need accurate information about the success of these policies. You would find it hard to succeed in your position were the principals in your district regularly to undermine your authority when they disagreed with your judgments. If you put yourself in the position of a board member, it is unlikely that you would be impressed with the argument that lying served good ends.

LYING AND BENEFIT MAXIMIZATION

Suppose that we apply the ideal of benefit maximization to the issue of lying to the school board. We are asked to consider whether lying might not be a good thing because it protects what all (in your school) agree is a good program from board policies that most (in your school) consider unwise. What are the consequences? Suppose that it is true that the children in your school will be better off if you mislead the board; does that decide the matter? There may be other consequences. For example, you must consider the effects of your behavior not only on the children in your school, but on the children in other schools. Perhaps your disregard for board policy will contribute to a climate in which other principals (perhaps less enlightened and more self-serving than yourself) will feel entitled to ignore board policy when they feel it is useful. You may weaken the board's authority with the result that the children in other schools are harmed because the board is unable to secure compliance with even sound policy.

Also consider that the board of education is an elected body; its authority is democratic authority, the authority of the people. Democratic authority does not exist if citizens decide that they will obey it only when they believe it is correct. When those who are employed to do the will of an elected body decide that they are free to substitute their judgment for that of the legislature should they deem it to be wrong, they erode the authority of the elected representatives of the people. Moreover, if the board cannot count on its principals to carry out its policies, it may need to generate more elaborate enforcement mechanisms. The district's organization may become more hierarchical, more rule-governed, and less collegial.

LYING AND COMMUNITY

Finally, consider the implications of your deception for your own school. Your willingness to lie to the board may ultimately erode the climate of trust in your school and its sense of community. While your authority in your school formally consists of the fact that you have been appointed to the role of principal, and that role carries with it certain powers, your ability to exercise this authority successfully depends on the fact that those who work under you trust your integrity and judgment. You should not be surprised if your willingness to lie to the board, even on the behalf of people in your school, is taken by those who work under you as a sign that you may also be willing to lie to them when you think it convenient.

Lies by public employees commonly have effects of this sort. When school leaders are not trusted by other members of the school community, the community changes. It becomes harder to achieve decisions by open discussion. People look out for their own interests rather than those of the school and its children. Your moral authority is eroded, and you will need to rely more on the formal authority that comes with your position and your ability to reward people for compliance. Behavior in the school becomes more rule-governed and bureaucratic and less purpose-driven and consensual. Solidarity is broken, and community eroded.

Your school community is an educational community. Truth-telling is essential to education. It is essential to the assessment of evidence. Not every fact can be directly checked by everyone to whom it is presented. Productive argument cannot proceed unless we trust the integrity of those with whom we argue. Teachers cannot teach unless their students believe that they are truthful. Truth-telling is essential to the educational process. Learning cannot occur where there is not confidence in the integrity of those who teach.

School leaders are not just administrators charged with the efficient operation of their schools. They are, in a sense, elders. An *elder* is someone whose authority rests on the fact that he or she exemplifies the virtues essential to the community. We expect clergy not only to be good preachers, but to be spiritual people. Similarly, we should expect that school leaders will exhibit those characteristics that are central to the educational process. These include respect for evidence and argument, and, perhaps above all, integrity and truth-telling. The school leader is the chief tone-setter and role model for the school. School leaders need to exemplify the virtues required by educational institutions.

Respect for persons and benefit maximization are bound up with the emphasis on truth-telling as essential to educational communities. Students are not respected if they are lied to not only because we would not wish to be lied to were we in their place, but because they cannot learn apart from an environment in which truth-telling is taken for granted. In a school where truth is not taken for granted and trust does not prevail, children are less likely to mature into the people we hope they will become—people who are able to reason and discuss. Lying has bad consequences because ultimately it is miseducative.

TRUST AND COMMUNITY

Lying erodes trust. Why is trust so important? (See Baier [1995].) Trust is important because it is a condition of community, and a sense of community is essential to good education. To see why trust is important, we need to consider why communities are important.

Communities exist to enable cooperation aimed at the achievement of certain shared goods. Political communities, for example, aim at justice and the common good. Religious communities may aim at such goods as faith, instruction of the young, worship, or righteousness. Intellectual communities aim at research, the pursuit of truth, and educating new members.

In addition to the goods that communities exist to pursue, they often produce other goods that are important to their members. A sense of belonging is one such good. Friendship is another.

One feature of community that is especially important to consider is that in communities, cooperation is more central than competition. This must be said carefully, so that it is not a mere platitude. Competition is a part of life and will be as long as resources are scarce. Moreover, in many contexts, competition is a virtue since it often elicits productivity and efficiency. Indeed, when competition is structured by shared understandings about its purposes and rules, it is a form of cooperation.

What makes communities different from other associations is not that competition is absent but that it is secondary. Consider orchestras or football teams. Members of orchestras compete for chairs and solos, and members of football teams for playing time. However, it is also important to note that orchestras and football teams must succeed or fail as a whole. Orchestras perform well or not as a unit; football teams can only win or lose as a team. Also, the excellence of each community member contributes to the excellence of the whole. If I am a violinist in an orchestra, my goal is that the orchestra should play well. This goal is enhanced if the oboist plays well. The oboist's success does not diminish my success if I identify this with the orchestra's playing well—it contributes to it.

This is also often true of intellectual and educational communities. If the goal is to advance knowledge through teaching or inquiry, the success of each contributes to the success of all. It is, for example, to my advantage as a scholar to have other able scholars in my department. I can learn from them, and they from me. In good academic departments, able scholars make one another better. The same thing is true in good classrooms and schools. When students learn with and from one another, the success of each can contribute to the success of all. When teachers are members of learning communities, what one teacher learns is a resource for others, and one teacher's success contributes to the advancement of goals shared by all.

Solidarity is essential to the functioning of healthy communities because solidarity is the basis of cooperation. Solidarity involves a commitment to the community's goals and to the members of the community. If members of the orchestra neither care about playing well nor value one another as members, they are unlikely to work or play well together.

Trust is essential, because when trust disappears, solidarity is difficult to maintain. Here, trust means something specific. When we trust other members of a community, it is not just that we believe they have such virtues as honesty or integrity. What we have confidence in is that they, like ourselves, are motivated by the goals of the community and by loyalty to its members. We trust them because we believe that they share our concerns. They want what we want. They, like ourselves, will subordinate personal goals to shared collective ones when they conflict.

The preceding suggests another reason why educators need to strive for clarity about the purposes a good education serves. Trust relies on the integrity of members of a community. But it also relies on the belief that members of a community are committed to its purposes. If they are to be so committed, they must understand what these purposes are.

Lying undermines community because it dissolves trust and, hence, solidarity. Lying signifies a failure of personal integrity. But it also signals the loss of commitment to the purposes of the community. When people lie, we can no longer be confident that they want what we want. Lying signifies that they are motivated by their own private and personal desires; hence, not by the goals of the community.

These considerations do not, I believe, show that it is never wrong to lie. There are, no doubt, cases of an extreme sort where lying is justified. I would not argue, for example, that in a just war we must not deceive our enemies or that we may not deceive people who propose to commit murder about the location of their victims. There may also be cases of a simpler sort (white lies) where lying is a simple kindness.

However, I think my arguments do strongly suggest that lying is unlikely to be a morally acceptable response in most of those cases where leaders are likely to be tempted to lie. Often when we believe that we are lying to achieve worthy goals, we will discover that we have failed to consider all of the relevant consequences, that we would have a different view were our roles exchanged with those to whom we are lying, and that we are squandering trust and eroding community. Honesty is the best policy almost all of the time. Leadership requires, before all else, integrity and a manifest commitment to the community's purposes. Lying abandons both.

CONCLUSIONS AND OUTLINE OF CHAPTERS

Ethics concerns the question, How shall we live well together? When we emphasize this as the central question, we are led to interpret the questions, What is good? and What is right? as questions about the nature of good communities. Good communities have worthy aims and a fair basis of cooperation. The role of the educational leader is to create good educational communities.

In what follows, I will trace this concern for good communities through six chapters. A brief description of each may help you to see how each contributes to understanding good educational communities.

In Chapter 2, I discuss the goals of education. I argue for four broad goals: students should become economically competent, become good citizens and moral people, be capable of an examined life, and discover ideas, activities, and relationships that enrich their lives. I suggest that these goals are big-tented and can serve as the goals of public schools.

Chapter 3 discusses two essential freedoms: intellectual and religious liberty. Here I am interested in discussing their role in creating good educational communities. I argue that the goals of education described in this chapter require that we create intellectual communities in our schools where free and open debate is cherished and protected. I also claim that we must give provisional authority to certain ideas because they are essential tools of thought. Finally, emphasizing the current debate about creationism and intelligent design, I discuss freedom of conscience and religious liberty and show why religious ideas cannot be given provisional authority in public schools.

In Chapter 4, I discuss equality of opportunity, resource allocation, and multicultural community. I argue that we are more likely to achieve equality of opportunity if our schools are able to achieve a sense of themselves as communities in which "we are all in this together," where the success of each is seen as contributing to the betterment of all, and where the weakest and most vulnerable are cared for.

In Chapter 5, I discuss the connections between the concepts of democracy, community, and accountability. I pay special attention to the conflict between different norms of legitimate authority and how these generate role conflicts for leaders with respect to accountability. I argue that accountability is not merely a matter of raising test scores. Leaders are accountable to professional standards and ideas and to members of the local community as well.

Chapter 6 discusses the ethics of decision making. I argue that there is an important distinction to be drawn between data- and evidence-driven decision making, and I argue for the latter. I also argue that a core idea for good educational organizations is that they need to institutionalize evidence-driven decision making in a way that makes it an ongoing collective responsibility. This chapter also connects the idea of due process to the idea of evidence-based decision making.

In Chapter 7, I turn explicitly to the ethics of accountability. There I argue that accountability has the potential to do good and to do harm. One of the things that makes a difference between doing good and doing harm is the existence of schools that are collectively reflective about the meaning of a good education and about how to provide it. Schools that are able to be collectively reflective about these things will be able not only to succeed, but to employ accountability measures to improve. Schools that are not collectively reflective are likely to succumb to the potential evils of accountability: gaming, goal erosion, and motivational displacement.

2

What Is Education For?

Our Nation is at risk. Our once unchallenged preeminence in commerce, industry, science, and technological innovation is being overtaken by competitors throughout the world. This report is concerned with only one of the many causes and dimensions of the problem, but it is the one that undergirds American prosperity, security, and civility. . . . What was unimaginable a generation ago has begun to occur—others are matching and surpassing our educational attainments.

—*A Nation at Risk* (National Commission
on Excellence in Education, 1983)

Let us hope . . . that by the best cultivation of the physical world beneath and around us, and the best intellectual and moral world within us, we shall secure an intellectual, social, and political prosperity and happiness, whose course shall be onward and upward, and which, while the earth endures, shall not pass away.

—Abraham Lincoln (Bartlett, 1955)

The unexamined life is not worth living.

—Socrates (Plato, 1928a)

Socratic argument . . . is essential to a strong democracy and to any lasting pursuit of justice. In order to foster a democracy that is reflective and deliberative, rather than simply a marketplace of competing interest groups, a democracy that takes thought for the common good, we must produce citizens who have the Socratic capacity to reason about their beliefs. . . . To unmask prejudice and to secure justice, we need argument, an essential tool of civic freedom.

—Martha Nussbaum (1997, p. 19)

But there is no known Epicurean theory of life that does not assign to the pleasures of the intellect, of the feelings and imagination, and of the moral sentiments, a higher value as pleasures than those of mere sensation.

—John Stuart Mill (Bentham & Mill, 1961, p. 408)

Hence: It is better to be a human being dissatisfied than a pig satisfied; better to be Socrates dissatisfied than a fool satisfied. And if the fool, or the pig, are of a different opinion, it is only because they only know their own side of the question.

—John Stuart Mill (Bentham & Mill, 1961, p. 410)

PROLOGUE AND SCENARIO

In the previous chapter, I suggested that one part of the argument of the parents and teachers in your school against the board of education's new policies was the claim that they amounted to drill and kill. I then suggested that the core of this objection was that the board's policies seemed to your teachers and parents to be inconsistent with a view of the aims of education that emphasizes understanding and involves reflection, argument, and the appraisal of evidence. This kind of knowledge, I suggested, is often connected with the ideals of character and citizenship.

To get a feel for these issues, I want to extend the scenario of the previous chapter.

You are the principal of a middle school in the same district I described in the first iteration of the scenario in Chapter 1. Your state requires testing in three areas at the end of eighth grade: reading, writing, and mathematics. Your school has agreed to participate in a study conducted by a nearby university. The study is concerned with the consequences of the board's policies that require a curriculum thoroughly aligned with state tests and that mandate a fair amount of "test prep." The question the study asked was, "How have these mandates changed instruction?" Here is what the researchers found.

1. Reading instruction shifted to include more reading of short passages. There was less reading of longer stories and less discussion of the ideas in these stories. The focus emphasized reading comprehension over analysis and interpretation.

2. *The teaching of writing moved from a focus on ideas and arguments to a focus on writing short essays with more attention paid to the internal structure of sentences and the organization of paragraphs. Writing assignments became more numerous and shorter. Students were taught to use rubrics to structure and evaluate their writing.*

3. *Mathematics instruction tended to involve fewer word problems and more practice doing calculations.*

4. *Less time was spent on art, music, and social studies.*

5. *There were some subtle changes over each of the three tested subject areas. The curriculum was less likely to "tell a story," that is, it was harder to see a coherent sequence of ideas being built over time in these areas. There were fewer uniting themes and more fragmentation. There was also less emphasis on inquiry. Even when there were word problems to be solved in mathematics, teachers were more likely to walk students through the problems than to engage in lengthy Socratic discussions about them. There was more emphasis on coverage. The curriculum became "less about more."*

The report concluded that these results suggested that teachers had done what the board asked them to do in a responsible way. Instructional changes resulted from the fact that the state gave tests in three areas: reading, writing, and mathematics. The reading test emphasized comprehension and employed many brief paragraphs. The writing test asked students to write a five-paragraph essay on a self-selected topic. Essays were scored using a rubric that was attentive to sentence structure and the essay's organization, but did not take content into consideration. Finally, the mathematics test emphasized calculations over word problems. The report also noted that this school's test scores had gone up.

WHAT SHOULD WE MAKE OF THIS?

A few things to note: First, these results do not suggest that district policy has inspired anything that might plausibly be described as drill and kill. Teachers have not started to use flash cards to teach mathematical facts, they have not started to give out long lists of vocabulary words with definitions to be memorized, and they have not started to have students memorize the answers to released tests, although they do review them. What has happened is not endless memorization and rote learning. The expression *drill and kill* has proven to be an inaccurate hyperbole. What has happened is that instruction has tended to emphasize comprehension and skill acquisition over analysis, discussion, interpretation, and argument.

There is nothing wrong with comprehension and skill acquisition. Indeed, they are prerequisites of a good education. Nevertheless, the question we should ask concerns whether anything is lost in these changes. Why should we care if there is less analysis, discussion, interpretation, and argument? Should we worry that there is less art, music, and social studies? Have the ideals of character and citizenship about which teachers and parents worried in the first iteration of our scenario been negatively impacted? Are there consequences for other worthy goals?

What is important about the arguments of the parents and teachers in my initial scenario is that they tap into educational ideals that, even if not well articulated, are nevertheless important to any school. They assert aims that are arguably fundamental to good educational communities, aims that must be discussed if we are to understand what living well together means in a school. In this chapter, I will develop a fuller picture of some of these aims. I will propose that a good education is attentive to the following four broad educational goals:

1. *Human capital development.* People need to have knowledge and skill to earn a living, and society requires people with a variety of knowledge and skills if it is to have an adequately productive economy.

2. *The examined life.* If people are not to be cognitive captives of their cultures, their traditions, or their untutored desires, they need the ability to reflect on their own lives.

3. *Citizenship.* People need to possess the knowledge, skills, and virtues required if they are to be citizens of a liberal democratic society.

4. *The cognitive prerequisites of human flourishing.* People need a praiseworthy view of good living and the cognitive skills required to lead such a life.

These goals all require high levels of cognitive development. They are, I would suppose, the kinds of goals that are promoted by analysis, discussion, interpretation, and argument. If the instructional program of your school begins to focus more on comprehension and skill acquisition, it may be less likely to succeed at such goals.

HUMAN CAPITAL DEVELOPMENT

What is education for? The opening paragraphs of *A Nation at Risk* (National Commission on Excellence in Education, 1983), quoted above, provide one answer. We are, it suggests, concerned with national prosperity and security.

So how does education contribute to national prosperity and security? The most obvious answer is that education develops human capital. *Capital* consists of resources that promote economic productivity; *human capital* is the portion that resides in human knowledge and skills. To say that education aims at the production of human capital is to say that education aims at the production of the kinds of knowledge and skill that have productive value. *A Nation at Risk* also tends to see human capital as a social interest (we want a prosperous society) more than an individual interest (we want good jobs for our children), but we should remind ourselves that it is both.

It is unquestionably true that education does and must develop human capital. The knowledge of how to make things and provide services is neither innate nor naturally acquired. If any generation failed to transmit its human capital to the next, civilization would end. We would starve.

But although the idea that education aims at producing and reproducing human capital is self-evidently true, it is also largely vacuous unless it is fleshed out. It does not tell us what kinds of human capital we need; nor does it tell us what kinds of institutions we need to reproduce human capital. After all, arguably the most important kind of human capital concerns the production of food. For much of history, the majority of human beings farmed for a living and transmitted the human capital required to do so informally—without the benefit of schools, and with little knowledge of reading, writing, or mathematics. In today's society, few of us farm, and those who do need knowledge and skills that can sometimes be complex and esoteric.

No doubt what *A Nation at Risk* meant is that we need to produce the kinds of human capital required by a modern technological economy (and military) that will enable the United States to be preeminent in commerce and defense, and we need good schools to do this. This view may still achieve wide agreement, but we can now begin to imagine that some will disagree. Perhaps we should disavow aspirations for the kind of prosperity that depends on the high consumption of goods and services in favor of a simpler life. (Some research suggests that the happiest people in the United States are the Amish, who have disavowed our high-tech society in favor of agrarian simplicity.) Others may question the need for the kind of military prowess the United States has achieved. And while it is clear that it is important for all people to produce enough to live well and be secure, it is less evident that we need the United States to be preeminent in commerce and defense.

Even if we grant that what we want is an educational system that produces prosperity and security as we commonly understand them, it is still not self-evident what kinds of knowledge the schools of our society need to promote. One example of the failure of the U.S. educational system I once heard from a prominent politician was the inability of many U.S. students to accurately locate the United States on a map of North America. But why is this knowledge required for prosperity or security? I feel that I should know this basic geography (and I do), and that others should know it as well. But I cannot say that I have ever needed to know this to perform any job I have had. Nor can I say that I have needed to know much more than that Canada is north and Mexico south to exercise my responsibilities as a citizen or to travel to Canada or to Mexico. I imagine this is true of most other people.

When we see an example of deplorable ignorance, we cannot just wring our hands, cry "prosperity and security," and assume that we have explained why people should know what they are now ignorant of. There are many ills education might cure: obesity, bad taste in clothing, sexual promiscuity, the inability to read Arabic, not knowing how to wire a circuit, and ignorance of the Irish potato famine. (New York, by the way, mandates study of the Irish potato famine.)

We cannot expect to cure every deficiency through education. If we respond willy-nilly to every piece of ignorance with an educational mandate, we will produce chaos and incoherence. We need to set priorities. If we are to develop curriculum on the assumption that we are attempting to increase human capital, we will need to carefully answer the following questions: Who needs to know what, and for what reason? and In what does human capital consist?

A Nation at Risk has generated an insistence that understands *accountability* to mean that schools should produce students whose achievement is satisfactory based on standards and measured by standardized tests. States have spent much time and effort in the past two decades developing standards and tests to measure whether students have met them. Perhaps, then, we might look to these standards and tests to determine what people believe to be the knowledge that society requires.

At the elementary-school level, tests characteristically emphasize reading and computation. *No Child Left Behind* (NCLB) (2002) mandates testing in these areas, with science (perhaps) to come. The graduation tests that are being put in place in some states tend to emphasize adequate mastery of algebra, history, writing, and science.

Here is an item (admittedly chosen for its arcane nature) from a recent exam in Earth Science, a requirement that New York students must meet if they are to graduate: "Which star's surface temperature is closest to the temperature at the boundary between earth's mantle and core?" (New York State Board of Regents, 2005). Are bits of knowledge such as this what human capital consists in? A thought experiment: Suppose the exit tests that are becoming required for high school graduation were given to the members of the state legislatures who have passed the legislation requiring them. How many legislators would pass? How many teachers would pass the exams in subjects they do not teach? I imagine that many would not pass.

If so, does this tell us that these people are deficient, or that mastery of these subjects is not really that essential to the development of the kinds of human capital our society requires? Is our nation at risk from such legislators and teachers? Do we value knowledge of these subjects because we believe the knowledge is retained, or because we believe that studying these subjects shapes values and creates capacities that are valuable even when detailed knowledge is lost? The latter seems to me to be a more reasonable view, but we often do not teach as though we believe it.

Consider some arguments in favor of a curriculum of the sort that the standards movement has generated. At the elementary level, this curriculum emphasizes basic skills, reading, composition, and computation. These central components of an elementary education are justified by several considerations. They are essential for almost all forms of participation in our society. To be unable to read, communicate, and do checkbook math is to be all but excluded from most of the economic and political institutions of our society. These skills are prerequisite for further education. They are also essential to the welfare of society as a whole. A society in which the majority (or a significant minority) of citizens are deficient in these skills is unlikely to be very prosperous or secure. In addition, it is unlikely to be very free or democratic.

Think of these skills as universal educational instrumentalities. It does not matter much what people want in life. They are unlikely to be able to attain their life goals if they cannot read, communicate, or compute at some minimally adequate level. Moreover, there are few social interests to which widespread mastery of such skills in not important. In our society, such universal educational instrumentalities are the fundamental form of human capital. Because they are so important, it seems to me to be entirely reasonable that schools should be accountable for teaching them and students for learning them.

Arguments of this sort do not work as well when we apply them to the kinds of knowledge that high schools seek to provide and states increasingly test for. The standards movement at the secondary level has emphasized academic knowledge—the kind of knowledge that historically, in our society, has been the province of elites and the prerequisite to college. When we emphasize academic learning at the expense of vocational education, we are substituting one form of human capital for another. Hence, we need an argument that suggests why academic subject matter (e.g., algebra, history, science, literature, composition, etc.) constitutes the primary form of human capital to be produced at the secondary level. And if we require these subjects of everyone, we will need an additional argument to show that everyone should be proficient in these matters. It is clear that our society needs many people who are good at algebra. It is less clear that all students should be good at algebra.

Consider a common argument employed here. We are increasingly a knowledge-based society. Jobs that do not require high levels of educational attainment are likely to be exported to low-wage countries. Societies that wish to maintain a high level of employment and collective prosperity and security need to compete with advanced knowledge and skills. Scientists, engineers, and other knowledge industry workers are the engines of economic progress and our collective security. Moreover, we need people who are capable of creativity and critical thinking. The kind of curriculum that is dominated by academic knowledge is the one best suited to producing the kinds of people our society needs.

I do not find this argument particularly convincing for the proposition that *everyone* needs to master a broad range of academic subjects. Since *A Nation at Risk* was written, we have had significant economic growth and, through the later 1990s, almost full employment. Yet there has been little real change in educational attainment. *Goals 2000* (1998), the signature educational legislation of the Clinton administration, boasted that we would be first in the world in science and mathematics by the year 2000. We are not. Nor have we moved up significantly in those international rankings that are the basis of so much anxiety. Moreover, as the flood of illegal immigration the United States is currently undergoing attests, there is considerable need for unskilled labor.

Nor have we had any more than spot shortages of knowledge workers. Those we have had have been made up for by immigration. And we have begun to outsource some of this knowledge work, not so much because we lack talented workers, but because others do this work cheaper. Japan, whose educational system was much admired in the United States only a few years ago and whose government once lectured us about the harmful effects of our poor educational system, has, by contrast, stagnated economically.

These facts do not cast doubt on the notion that we are a knowledge society and that our prosperity and security depend on an adequate supply of knowledge workers. They do cast doubt on the notion that there is a simple and direct connection between a curriculum of a certain sort and economic prosperity, and especially on the notion that this curriculum should be a standard one required of all.

I have not made these arguments because I oppose the standards movement or strong academic requirements for high school graduation. I have made them because I believe that, while it is clear that there is a connection of some sort between good schools and prosperity and security, the nature of this connection is neither simple nor clear. Once we get past the need for a basic education, human capital arguments claiming that *all* students need a rigorous academic education are, at best, conjectural. I have wanted to create a little doubt about the kind of rhetoric that seems to dominate so much educational discourse so as to open up some space to consider other views concerning what education is for beyond the creation of human capital. There are other matters to consider.

THE EXAMINED LIFE

Socrates is credited by Plato (1928a) with the saying, "The unexamined life is not worth living." For Socrates, this was not an idle pronouncement. He was executed by an Athenian court for his educational practices. We might begin to understand his claim by recounting the story of the trial of Socrates as told by Plato in *The Apology.*

Socrates described himself as a gadfly—an annoying insect. He claimed to lack any special wisdom or knowledge and, if he were wise (the Oracle at Delphi had pronounced him the wisest of men), his wisdom consisted of the fact that he knew he lacked knowledge while others did not. Socrates spent much of his life in the Athenian marketplace engaged in discussion with those who wished to talk with him. Often his interlocutors were the young men of Athens, especially those from elite families. Socrates is represented as asking them questions and interrogating their answers.

The questions Socrates addressed were among the fundamental questions of human life: What is justice? What is love? What is virtue? What is piety? What is good? What is knowledge? Can virtue be taught? and How shall we live? Plato, who wrote many dialogues in which Socrates is the primary figure, eventually gave answers to many of these questions via Socrates's mouth. Because we know little about Socrates apart from these dialogues, distinguishing Socrates from Plato is not always easy. Yet it is likely that Socrates was tried and executed, not so much for the answers he gave as for the questions he asked and the manner in which he pursued them.

For example, in the dialogue *Euthyphro* (Plato, 1928b), Socrates addresses the question of the nature of religious piety. He is concerned with the answer because he has just been put on trial for impiety. He approaches a man who was known in Athens for his piety, Euthyphro, and asks him to explain what piety is. Socrates eventually constructs the following paradox: Either what is right is right because the gods love it, or the gods love what is right because it is right. Neither answer is satisfactory. If something is right because the gods love it, then anything might be right, for the gods might love anything. What they love will depend only on their will, which is arbitrary. If, however, the gods love what is right because it is right, then what is right is right apart from the fact that the gods love it. If so, we do not need knowledge of the gods to know what is right.

Euthyphro's response to Socrates's questions is largely one of irritation and impatience. Socrates was tried, condemned, and executed (by drinking hemlock) for impiety and corrupting the youth. Socrates lived in a society that, like ours, was increasingly multicultural, increasingly aware that human beings answer life's persistent questions in quite different ways, and increasingly insecure about its own commitments.

The questions Socrates asked were not merely academic questions. As is the case for us, people felt a stake in how they were answered. Some wished to assert the time-honored answers of Athenian culture and religion. Others questioned these answers and asserted different ones. The charges of impiety and corrupting the youth were brought by those who feared that Socratic inquiry would erode the traditional moral foundations of Athens, a fear that was well founded.

Socratic inquiry creates a tension between reason and tradition. How will we know that we have attained the right answers to our questions? Socrates's answer is that we know that we have correctly answered our questions, not when we know the answers favored by our culture, but when the answers we give have been given a convincing argument that has withstood searching criticism.

Reason versus tradition? A number of comments are in order about this. Nothing about Socratic inquiry requires that one abandon one's traditions. What is required is that one test them. Abandonment is required only if a tradition cannot meet the test of reason. Moreover, as we shall see in the next chapter, some level of respect for traditions is a requirement of inquiry. We should not forget that our various cultures and traditions are not only potential objects of criticism, they are the sources of people's identities and provide the cognitive resources that make criticism and reflection possible.

Sometimes Socratic inquiry is linked to Cartesian doubt. René Descartes (1956) wanted to begin the process of creating knowledge anew by wiping the slate clean. Received knowledge, Descartes claimed, was nothing more than a mass of conjecture and prejudice. We should not, he suggested, accept any idea until it has been proven. We should doubt all and start over. My view of Socratic inquiry does not involve Cartesian doubt. It respects traditions while also recognizing that it is critique that makes progress possible and permits people to live their lives freely from the inside.

If Socratic inquiry is to make sense as a personal ideal, it must be accompanied by what we might call a constructive project. If people are to be asked to question their traditions and occasionally modify and abandon them, it must be possible to replace them with commitments that can meet the test of reason. Educators who encourage their students to undertake Socratic inquiry should keep this in mind. One is not primarily trying to undermine current conviction. One is attempting to help students live well by helping them to make good and justifiable choices about how they (and we) will live.

It is important that we not set the standard for reasonable choice unreasonably high. The philosophical tradition (beginning with Plato) has sometimes claimed that true knowledge requires more than adequate evidence. It requires certainty. However, when one is concerned to discover the nature of good human living, certainty is too high a standard, one that is unlikely ever to be met. What we should hope to help our students achieve is a conception of their lives that is reasonable and satisfactory to them and that rests on assumptions that can be defended. Because the question, How shall I live? is difficult, we should accept the probability that thoughtful people will come to different conclusions. The idea is not to ensure that students achieve the right conclusions or the same conclusions, but that they achieve conclusions that seem to them to be justifiable.

Here we may have at least three objectives: One is to help students choose a satisfactory life that they can live from the inside. The second is to help them avoid a life of servility before the traditions and norms of their society. The third is to enable democratic dialogue about our collective life.

I imagine that this discussion will make school leaders a bit uneasy. Socratic inquiry is not valued by all in our society. Criticism may come from both the right and the left—from those who see Socratic inquiry as a challenge to either faith or traditional American verities, and from those who view cultural critique as inconsistent with multiculturalism and a plurality of identities. Thus, those who encourage Socratic dialogue may be accused of the crimes of which Socrates was accused (impiety and corrupting the youth), as well as the more modern sins of domination and oppression.

Many in our society believe that it is not the responsibility of the public school to call into question the traditions and cultural norms of its many communities. While I think it is true that schools should not feel an entitlement to assault any culture or religion and, in a religiously diverse and culturally pluralistic society, that any discussion of these topics must be handled with great care and sensitivity, at the same time schools must be able to tell the truth, address questions about what counts as good human living, and consider issues relevant to the lives of their students. They cannot do these things if they must avoid anything that opens issues that may lead to cultural or religious critique.

Finally, some in our society seem to believe that Socratic inquiry is a waste of time and that we should get on with the task of creating human capital without its distraction. It is, perhaps, these people who are most in need of Socratic inquiry because they hold an impoverished view of life and are servile to the spirit of the age.

CITIZENSHIP

Few would deny that schools have an obligation to create good democratic citizens and decent and humane individuals. What this means is a more complex matter. We might have a minimalist conception. Perhaps good people and good citizens are those who abide by a shared morality. They don't lie or steal. They vote and obey the law.

If we want more of good citizens, we might also ask that people be community-spirited, that they volunteer to work for charitable or civic organizations, and that they treat one another with decency and respect. Another expansion of our conception of citizenship might involve hoping that citizens would be politically active. We might wish them to take an interest in public affairs, join advocacy groups, work for causes, and express their views. No doubt, all of these things are desirable. And we should note that one cannot be a good citizen without being a moral person. Citizenship incorporates morality.

If we are to have an even more robust view of citizenship for a democratic society, we should begin by asking what we mean by a *democratic society*. Consider two popular notions: The first is that a democratic society is one where the government rests on the consent of the governed. Commonly it is believed that this notion requires people to recognize the sovereignty of an elected legislature. The consent of the governed is expressed by institutions that permit people to vote for those who represent them. These views were asserted by the seventeenth-century philosopher John Locke (1960), whose *Second Treatise on Civil Government* was, perhaps, the most important source of ideas and ideals underlying the American system of government.

A second formulation, provided by Abraham Lincoln in his Gettysburg Address, holds that democracy is government of the people, by the people, and for the people. This adds to Locke's formulation an element of participation.

Both Locke's and Lincoln's formulations are rooted in a view that human beings are equal. Neither Locke nor Lincoln understood this to mean that every human being is the same as every other. Their ideal of equality does not, for example, deny individual differences in capacity. What both wish to deny is that any individual should be privileged over any other merely by circumstances of birth. No one is born with a right to rule or an obligation to serve. No one is born with a right to preferential treatment. These ideas and ideals can be viewed as an expression of the principle of equal respect.

Suppose, then, we say that a democratic society is one with institutions and practices that follow two basic rules: (1) everyone's interests are equal, and therefore everyone has an equal right to have his or her interests fairly considered in decision making; and (2) everyone has an equal right to have a fair influence on decisions.

Societies with elected legislatures that respect such norms as one person, one vote are thought to respect these basic democratic norms. This is not, however, inevitably the case. Imagine, for example, a society in which a majority managed to achieve dominance over the legislature and used this dominance to pursue its interests at the expense of the minority. Such a society might routinely elect a legislature and permit participation in voting by members of the minority. Nevertheless, it might be characterized as a tyranny of the majority and, thus, not adequately democratic.

This comment suggests that a genuinely democratic society is characterized by a search for the common good. What might we mean by the *common good*? Here are some things we do not mean: Common goods are not goods owned in common. Nor, in seeking the common good, should we assume that everyone should want the same things or value the same kind of life. Nor should we mean by the common good what some economists appear to mean. The common good is more than goods that are not adequately satisfied by free markets and thus must be provided by government. Let me suggest another definition: The common good is those goods which members of a democratic society decide to pursue, either collectively or as individuals, once they have fairly considered the interests of their fellow citizens. The core of the idea is that in democratic societies, the people rule in the interest of all.

Suppose that I am considering the purchase of a new car. What kind of car do I want? I may ask certain questions to make a decision: What can I afford? What size car do I want or need? Do I need all-wheel drive? Do I care about power, styling, comfort, or convenience? These questions all reference the decision to my wants. If, however, I care about the common good, I must ask other questions. Does this car pollute the air other people breathe? Does it consume too much gasoline so that the price others must pay becomes beyond their means? Does it deplete the store of fossil fuel so that future generations must go without? Is it safe—not just for me, but for others? If I am to consider the common good, I must reference my decisions not only to my needs, but to those of others as well.

We are now in a position to understand the point of the quotation from Martha Nussbaum (1997) and the connection between citizenship and Socratic dialogue that she sees. Nussbaum, recall, wants a democracy in which deliberation is central. To see her point, consider an alternative view: One might view a democratic society and democratic politics as a means whereby individuals compete to satisfy their own interests in a nonviolent and fair way. Your interests and mine conflict. Wants are infinite, resources finite. We are in competition to satisfy our wants.

Democratic politics provides a nonviolent way to engage in this competition. We elect people who will represent our interests. Others do likewise. If those we elect are to be able to pass legislation, it is likely that they will have to work out a compromise. You will get something of what you want, but not all. So will I. Viewing democratic politics in this way is to see it as a kind of power struggle among individuals or groups, each of whom wishes to get as much for themselves as possible. Democratic government "vectors" competing interests.

Nussbaum distinguishes this view from a view of democracy that seeks for the common good. If democracy is a kind of power struggle, we need only to know and consider our own good. But if democracy is the pursuit of the common good, then we must know and consider not only our interests, but those of others.

Nussbaum notes the connection of this conception of democracy with Socratic dialogue. If we are to seek for the common good, we must value reason and dialogue. Indeed, we must do no less than examine our lives in concert with others. To seek for the common good is to examine what we take to be our interests and ask if they are consistent with the common good, and to change our conception of what we want if it cannot meet this test.

As educators, if we accept the view that we should be engaged in educating citizens for the kind of democratic society that Nussbaum proposes, we must address the task of helping to create in our students the knowledge, capacities, and values that support such an enterprise. Here, too, tradition may be respected, but not in a servile way. We must also be willing to consider and come to understand the traditions of others (see Callan, 1997). And we must be prepared to offer and accept criticism in our pursuit of the common good.

Developing citizens who are able to do these things is a daunting and threatening task that requires the wisdom and skill of the school leader. Many in our society will not value an education in which what they want or the traditions they prize are subject to criticism. They will want schools to promote their view or be silent. Again, I am not suggesting that schools engage in an assault on anyone's core values. Yet these values must be on the table for discussion. The pursuit of the common good is not possible if we are unwilling to engage in such argument. Schools that are so conflict-avoidant that difficult matters cannot be debated are not preparing democratic citizens.

HUMAN FLOURISHING

It remains to discuss Mill (Bentham & Mill, 1961). Mill is not tactful. His comments make a distinction between the higher and lower pleasures, he characterizes these as pleasures of the intellect, and he compares those who think otherwise as fools and pigs: "Better a Socrates dissatisfied than a fool satisfied." His views are easily seen as those of an intellectual snob (possibly because this is true). While we might grant that Mill's writings do not meet the standards of a more egalitarian age, I want to put before you the case that he is essentially correct and that one can understand his views in a way that is not elitist.

What kind of life is a good life? Because we live in a liberal democratic society where people are presumed to be entitled to have and pursue their own conception of good living so long as they respect the rights of others, educators need to take care how they answer such questions. If educators are to be guided by some conception of human flourishing, this conception needs to have certain features. It must be consistent with basic democratic values. It must not claim that there is one best way to live that is mandatory for all. A conception of good living must be big-tented in the sense that it is consistent with the diverse range of religions and cultures in our society. Moreover, it should explain in some measure what it is about diverse activities and practices that allows people to experience them as worthwhile.

Have we learned anything as yet about the nature of human flourishing? Is what we have learned consistent with these standards? We have looked at the Socratic maxim, "The unexamined life is not worth living."

I have said that part of the idea of an examined life is that we should not adopt every custom and tradition of our group uncritically. Rather, we must examine these customs and traditions. What makes this part of human flourishing?

Part of leading an examined life is seeking a life that is genuinely good for us. We should not assume that the good of each person consists of precisely the same thing. We have different tastes and talents. Our cultures and traditions shape us in such a way that we experience the world differently. That we should examine these traditions and cultures does not change the fact that they have made us into people who will find certain things satisfying. That people from different cultures prefer different foods is one obvious example.

The book of Proverbs in the Old Testament states, "Train up a child in the way that he should go, and when he is old he will not depart from it." This passage can be read in two different ways. We can insist that there is one way for all to find, and that children must find it early if they are to stay on the right path. But we may also emphasize the idea that for each individual there is a way that he or she should go that must be found. Finding that way is part of the examined life. Why, then, is the examined life part of human flourishing? Because if we examine our lives, we are more likely to find that way of living that is right for us than if we blindly follow custom and tradition (see Brighouse, 2000).

A second reason is suggested by Mill. It is better, Mill says, to be Socrates dissatisfied than a fool satisfied. Why? One reason may be that those who live the examined life come to have capacities and virtues that they value in themselves. Imagine someone who has developed the capacities required to reflect on his or her life. This person may have struggled with many choices and experienced uncertainty. Life may have involved some failed experiments and false starts. There may have been some dissatisfaction. Perhaps this person has chosen a path that has estranged friends and loved ones. Can one imagine such a person stating, "I wish I had remained an unreflective person. I wish that instead of seeking a life that was best for me, I had adopted without reflection the life that my community or my parents lived or the life that they urged on me. I wish I had remained subservient and servile before the wishes of others." Mill's conjecture may be that those who have become the kinds of people who are able to lead an examined life will find the person they have become admirable—a source of pride and pleasure—and will not, therefore, willingly become someone unreflectively ruled by custom and tradition. They value the kind of person they have become. Being this kind of person is part of human flourishing.

There is another aspect of Mill's view to consider. Mill may be proposing an answer to the question, What is it about various human activities and experiences that makes them enjoyable? Mill says that the greatest pleasures are those of the intellect. I believe that this is a half-truth. To see why and to explore Mill's idea, I want to consider two passages from two contemporary philosophers.

John Rawls (1971, p. 426) answers the question of what it is that makes activities and experiences enjoyable with what he refers to as the Aristotelian Principle: "Other things being equal, people enjoy the exercise of their realized capacities (their innate or trained abilities), and this enjoyment increases the more the capacity is realized, or the greater its complexity." Rawls is pointing out two things. First, people tend to enjoy doing what they are good at. Second, when they have a choice between two activities, they generally enjoy the one that calls more on their capacities and requires more complicated and subtle judgments. Rawls illustrates this by comparing chess and checkers. Someone who is able to play both with reasonable skill will generally prefer to play chess because it is the more complex game and evokes a higher level of capacity than does checkers. We might say something similar about music. People are more likely to enjoy listening to or performing music when doing so requires discernment and skill—provided, of course, that they have acquired the capacity for such discernment and skill.

We should note three things about these ideas. First, this view suggests that those activities that are most likely to satisfy over time require people to master a range of skills that enable performance and appreciation. We cannot enjoy doing what we cannot do, and we cannot appreciate experiences that we lack the capacity to experience. However, the Aristotelian Principle does not involve a preference for activities that are purely theoretical. Those activities that elicit pleasure may include intellectual activity along with art, literature, and music, but they also include activities such as craft and sport. Woodworkers and goldsmiths can meet the requirements of the Aristotelian Principle. Indeed, cooking and eating may also require skill and discernment: It is one thing to stuff one's face and another to savor a well-prepared meal and good wine. Thus, the range of activities that satisfy the Aristotelian Principle is quite wide.

Second, there is no cultural bias involved in this view. The Aristotelian Principle can be satisfied by activities of quite diverse sorts. Most cultures may be presumed to have invented activities that will meet its requirements.

Finally, learning to perceive is an important part of learning what is enjoyable about an activity. This last point can be illustrated by sports. A sport cannot be experienced as a sport at all without some learning. If we do not know the rules and the point of baseball, we cannot see home runs and strikeouts. We can only see people trying to hit white spheres with long sticks. We must learn to see hitting a white sphere over a fence with a stick as a home run. When we understand not only the rules and the point but are able to grasp the strategy and the subtleties of play also, we are able to see and enjoy more, even if we are only spectators. The more we understand, the more we can see; thus, the more we can appreciate and enjoy.

Consider the following remarks by Alasdair MacIntyre (1981), who is characterizing what he calls a *practice* as

> any coherent and complex form of socially established cooperative human activity through which goods internal to that form of activity are realized in the course of trying to achieve those standards of excellence which are appropriate to, and partially definitive of, that form of activity, with the result that human powers to achieve excellence, and human conceptions of the ends and goods involved, are systematically extended. (p. 175)

Examples of practices include complex games and sports (e.g., chess and football), academic disciplines (e.g., mathematics and biology), the arts (e.g., musical performance, dancing, and painting), many occupations (e.g., farming and engineering), and most crafts (e.g., pottery and making wooden canoes).

MacIntyre's notion of a practice and the view of what makes activities enjoyable is consistent with that of Rawls. But it adds several things that we should carefully attend to. It emphasizes the social character of practices. Practices such as mathematics, dance, and canoe making are activities that we learn from and engage in with others. Human beings do not learn by inventing the world anew. They learn largely by participating in those activities that other human beings have invented and have found worthwhile. Moreover, the social character of practices is a part of what makes them enjoyable. Doing with is better than just doing. Second, participation in these practices enables human beings to realize certain goods that could not be realized apart from mastery of the practices. Finally, the realization of these goods depends on mastery of various excellences that are required by the practice if we are to realize the goods that are internal to the practice.

These points can be illustrated by playing in an orchestra. We learn music by participating in an activity that was invented by others. The enjoyment of the music consists not only in playing it, but in playing it with others. And we enjoy playing more as we and others improve our skills.

Even activities done in solitude have their social aspects. For example, I build small boats in my woodshop. The skills involved were invented by and learned from others (even when they were learned from an instruction book). Discussing my progress with others adds to the enjoyment, as does attending places where others display their craft (and crafts).

We need to be careful not to interpret the idea that mastery of the excellences of a practice enables us to realize the goods of the practice in too instrumental a way. If we are successful at certain practices, we may be paid for engaging in them. Thus, income is a good that we may realize by mastery of a practice. In many cases, to master a practice is to develop human capital. But often human capital development and income are not the primary aims of a practice.

Consider poetry. Why should anyone care for poetry? The answer cannot be one to which human capital formation is central. There are few good jobs to be had by writing poetry. No doubt some people will earn money by writing verses for greeting cards and a few may earn a lot of money by writing song lyrics, but the aspiration for such positions is hardly a satisfactory reason for studying poetry for most people. Yet there are other goods to which poetry may lead. If we master its excellences, we may be able to appreciate the beauty of the language. Or poetry may help us to see the world in new and different ways. Or it may evoke powerful feelings. These are the goods that are internal to poetry.

When we master a practice, we are changed by it. Often the goods that are realized through practices are not fully comprehensible to those who have not attained some degree of mastery. Mathematicians and scientists often describe equations as elegant, powerful, or beautiful. Sometimes they may experience awe at the intricacies of nature and in their ability to "think God's thoughts after Him." Their experience of these creations is aesthetic. It is akin to the experience others may achieve by viewing a Rembrandt painting, hearing a Mozart symphony, or watching a well-executed pick-and-roll.

These are experiences and feelings that one cannot have apart from some degree of mastery of a practice. One need not be a great musician or composer to appreciate Mozart, but Mozart is more likely to be appreciated by those who have studied music or achieved some competence in performance. Practices are not only means to experiencing goods. They change us so that we become the kinds of people who are able to appreciate such goods.

These comments are not just about the arts; rather, they show that there can be art in everything. There are goods internal to the most practical of occupations. Farmers may experience pleasure in sifting rich soil through their fingers, and they will know things about the soil that others will not. My son, for example, is an engineer. His work concerns optimizing the supply chain for a company that manufactures a range of consumer products. This is, he tells me, a complex mathematical art. He has sent me papers that I have read with only modest comprehension, and has shown me spreadsheets and pointed to how the data entered disperse their consequences through complex equations and into output.

He is, I sometimes think to myself, essentially shipping sandpaper. Despite the fact that I am a woodworker and do have reasons to appreciate those who ensure that my hardware store has an adequate supply, I find that I am not much moved by the practical importance of this work. Nor is he! I doubt that he experiences great joy when his father reports that he was able to find just enough of the right grit. He is motivated by the elegance of his equations and by the challenge of their design. Like many good engineers, he enjoys puzzle solving, takes pleasure in using his skills, and appreciates a design well-conceived. He is unaffected by the fact that the sandpaper arrives just in time for his father's next project. Sometimes he wishes that I were able to see what he sees in his designs. Alas, I cannot.

If we cannot fully understand what goods are to be realized through practices, how are we to know what practices we should wish to master? Why not be satisfied with the more mundane pleasures that we are able to appreciate without significant effort? Two answers: First, we must trust the experience of others. The good teacher cannot immediately demonstrate the value of his or her practice to the novice student. He or she can only say, "Others who have mastered this art or this science have found that it enriches their lives. If you will allow me to teach you and to show you what others have found in it, you too may experience what they have experienced."

Second, not every person will enjoy every practice. I have found that Mozart enriches my life, and I am willing to climb a mountain for the sake of the view to be had at the top. But despite the occasional attempt, I do not much enjoy looking at paintings and (despite the preceding illustration) I do not particularly enjoy poetry. An annual trip to the art museum more than satisfies my need for art. Picasso, Monet, and Warhol are pretty much the same to me. I would much rather watch a well-played basketball game. Perhaps this is a character flaw, but I think the lesson to be learned is that the enjoyment of the goods internal to practices depends not only on the nature of the practice, but on the predispositions and capacities of the individual. I play several instruments with modest success. As a youth I was a good basketball player. My occasional attempts at poetry and painting have not been noteworthy for their success. The point is not that everyone should come to enjoy the same things—it is that everyone should master some things that they can enjoy.

Educators should not expect or hope to succeed with every student in every endeavor. The task is rather to do the best we can to ensure that all children find something of worth that engages their attention and in which they take pleasure. What individuals need in their education is a fair chance to discover which practices enrich their lives and which do not. What is needed, then, are good teachers who are able to show students what there is to be experienced in their practices, and the opportunity to meaningfully experience a range of practices so as to be able to discover those that fit.

I want to consider one more element of human flourishing. Human beings need and enjoy relationships with other human beings. Families are important to people. Friendship is a great good. Exercising the role of citizen can be the source not only of good government, but of friendships created through shared endeavors.

The mastery of practices is often the source of close friendships and meaningful relationships. I have sung in a number of community choruses and church choirs. I enjoy the music and take pleasure in learning and performing it, but I am at best a mediocre singer and this is not why I join. It is rather that I have enjoyed the associations that these choirs have provided. It is something I do with my wife. Choir members often become our friends. They are "our kind of people," and rehearsals involve interactions with others that I enjoy. Let me put the point of these observations into two aphorisms:

1. *Engaging in practices involves membership in a community.* Practices are social activities. They are sustained by the activities of members. They are acquired from others and done with others. Activity often involves cooperation toward shared ends. Performing groups and sports teams are, perhaps, paradigmatic of such shared activities built around a practice. Many readers will recall that some of their most meaningful and enduring friendships were formed around band, orchestra, choir, football, or basketball. Mastery of practices, then, may be valued not only because of the goods it enables us to realize, but the relationships it enables us to develop.

2. *Enjoyment of a practice is enhanced when it is done with someone.* I enjoy concerts and sports, but I do not enjoy going alone. I may even enjoy a trip to the art museum if it is a trip with someone whom I care about. Sharing experiences enhances them. Sharing them with someone we care about enhances them even more.

These two points suggest that when we are considering the value of the mastery of practices to the quality of life, we must be attentive to how important they are to our relationships with others.

CONCLUSIONS

I have argued that there are (at least) four central goals of education: human capital development, the capacity for an examined life, citizenship, and the development of those capacities that enhance experience. What kind of curriculum does this require? What kind of teaching does this require? Three worthwhile conclusions can be drawn from this discussion.

First, education should emphasize cognitive development. Our children should grow in their capacity to reason, assess evidence, deliberate with others about common goals, appreciate what is genuinely worthwhile, and understand and appreciate the views and cultures of others. Cognitive development is a kind of intersection where all these goals meet.

This observation includes human capital development. The kind of workforce we want is one in which people are flexible and have the ability to learn on the job and to learn a new job. We also want people who can appreciate the work that they do and who do work they can appreciate. We need to emphasize the "art" in occupations, and we should view the process of finding work that is satisfying to be a part of leading an examined life. Finally, we want people to see their work from the perspective of their role as citizens. This means not only that they should understand that honest work contributes to the well-being of others, but that people should be able and willing to assess the work they do with an eye to the common good as well as personal advancement.

Second, the education we offer our young people should be consistent with pluralism and individual variability. People have different capacities and come from different cultures. No one-size-fits-all education will provide the variability required to enable people to discern the life that is good for them. Moreover, a good education provides the opportunity to explore a range of human practices: art, music, sport, and craft need to be there along with academic subjects. Once basic knowledge and skills are developed and students begin to form an understanding of the direction they wish to go in life, there should be the opportunity for them to take different paths.

Third, the cultural opportunities that public schools offer need to be big-tented enough to accommodate the diversity of our diverse society. Music might serve as an example. Students need to be able to learn to appreciate the music of their own cultures and that of others. I would suggest three basic guidelines. While the music that is taught may reflect who is in a given school, students in any particular school should not experience the music curriculum as an act of cultural or religious domination. Second, the goal should be to learn to appreciate what is best in the various musical traditions explored, not simply to reinforce the preferences students bring with them to school. Finally, students should come to appreciate the traditions of others as well as what they see as their own.

I will conclude with a few comments on the implications of these ideas with respect to two of the themes of this book, community and accountability. Implicit in these goals is a commitment to at least two forms of community, intellectual community and democratic and multicultural community. The nature of these communities will be themes to explore, particularly in the next three chapters. Second, these ideas suggest three things we should be careful to avoid as we seek to make schools accountable:

1. *We should seek to be accountable in ways that emphasize cognitive development.* The parents and teachers in our initial scenario have argued that the board's policies promote rote learning, which they have dubbed with the cliché drill and kill. Is this true? It is an accusation often leveled at accountability programs that rely on high-stakes testing.

   In the modified scenario with which I began this chapter, I suggested that the drill and kill accusation may be overstated. Perhaps what is more likely to result from the board's policy is a shift in instructional strategy from an emphasis on argument and analysis to one that focuses more on comprehension and skill acquisition. What we can say is that if the board's policy does encourage an excess of rote learning that tends to undermine cognitive growth, that is a bad thing. And a move away from analysis and argument and toward comprehension and skill acquisition is at least suspect. It is a step away from the cognitive requirements of the goals I have outlined above. It may not be your privilege to disobey board policy, but it is your obligation to implement it in a way that is consistent with a more praiseworthy set of aspirations.

2. *We should seek to be accountable in ways that respect the need for a broad and flexible education for all.* Is high-stakes testing inconsistent with this? For example, New York requires that all students take and pass five tests in different subjects to graduate. Does this narrow the curriculum unacceptably? Does it push some students into dropping out? The scenario with which I began this chapter suggested that art and music were losing curricular space in the middle school. Is this occurring frequently? Is it acceptable? These are currently debatable matters. Here one should note that the subjects with which New York's tests are associated are only a fraction of any student's total educational experience. They do not, of themselves, amount to a one-size-fits-all education. Perhaps, then, the crucial question concerning such requirements is what you and your school will do with them. What will you do to succeed or to enable your students to succeed? What will you sacrifice so far as the breadth and flexibility of the education you offer is concerned?

3. *We should seek to be accountable in ways that avoid cultural dominance and that remain big-tented.* In Chapter 6, I will discuss a scenario concerning a high school that has emphasized African American history because there are many African American students in the school and because this is part of an attempt to create a multicultural community. I suggest that this emphasis has taken a toll on how well students do on their state's test in American history. Is this a problem? There is much to be said about this as a matter of policy (which I will not say). The matter is, I believe, debatable. What is important here is your reaction to the problem. How will you address the demands placed on you and still offer the program you think is best for your students?

If your school is to be a good school, you must view test results as a measure but not as the meaning of a good education. This means that you and your school community must interpret the meaning of test results, and to do that you need a defensible conception of the kind of education you wish to provide. The four goals I have discussed provide a framework for such a conception.

3

Constitutional Essentials, Part I

Intellectual Liberty, Religious Freedom, and Intellectual Community

Congress shall make no law respecting an establishment of religion, or prohibiting the free exercise thereof; or abridging the freedom of speech, or of the press; or the right to the people to peaceably assemble, and to petition the Government for a redress of grievances.

—First Amendment, U.S. Constitution

The vigilant protection of constitutional freedoms is nowhere more vital than in the community of American schools. The classroom is peculiarly the "marketplace of ideas." The Nation's future depends upon leaders trained through wide exposure to that robust exchange of ideas which discovers truth "out of a multitude of tongues" [rather] than through any kind of authoritative selection.

—*Keyishian v. Board of Regents*
(quoted in *Tinker v. Des Moines*, 1969)

He who lets the world . . . choose his plan of life for him has no need of any other faculty than the ape-like one of imitation. He who chooses his plan for himself employs all his faculties. He must use observation to see, reasoning and judgment to foresee, activity to gather materials for decision, firmness and self-control to hold to his deliberate decision. And these qualities he requires and exercises exactly in proportion as the part of his conduct which he determines according to judgment and feeling is a large one.

—John Stuart Mill (1859/1956) pp. 71–72)

PROLOGUE

I will begin this chapter by developing a conception of what I call *constitutional essentials*. Constitutional essentials are the core convictions of a political community. They are the political community's most basic answers to the question, How shall we live well together? The task of this chapter and the next two is to develop understandings of these constitutional essentials that are appropriate for an educational community and that serve the broad educational goals discussed in Chapter 2. If you are going to develop your school into a strong and healthy educational community, an understanding of the educational meaning of these constitutional essentials is crucial.

In this chapter, two constitutional essentials are discussed. I develop a conception of freedom of thought and expression that explores the educational role of dialogue and debate. I also note that an educational conception of intellectual liberty has to respect the provisional authority of certain core ideas because these ideas function as tools of thought and inquiry in some field of practice.

I also discuss freedom of religion. I argue that despite the fact that the exploration of religious ideas might seem an important part of the examined life, there are other values involved that schools must consider. These are freedom of conscience and the avoidance of civil strife. These values suggest that while educators should deal with subjects (such as history) that bear on an examination of religious ideas and, in these contexts, discussion of religious ideas should not be avoided, educators in public schools are well advised to avoid direct attempts to examine religious conceptions. Direct instruction concerning religion poses an excessive risk to freedom of conscience and promotes civil strife. Moreover, public schools may not give any provisional authority to religious conceptions.

Let's begin with a current issue. A few years ago the Supreme Court considered a Louisiana statute that required equal time for scientific creationism and evolution in the state's biology classes (see *Edwards v. Aguillard*, 1987). This law appealed to certain notions of fairness that are reasonably thought to be important to good education. It said that evolution is controversial. Many people in the United States believe the account of creation taught in the book of Genesis in the Bible, and they reject evolution. How shall we deal with this controversy in the classroom? "Present the evidence for both sides and let students make up their own minds," said the Louisiana law.

The Supreme Court rejected this view, claiming that the Louisiana law was not religiously neutral and that it violated the Establishment Clause of the First Amendment. Isn't the classroom supposed to be a marketplace of ideas? The Supreme Court said it was in the passage from *Tinker v. Des Moines* (1969) quoted above. Are not religious beliefs ideas? Why not put them on the table for discussion? Why restrict what students can be taught to one side of an argument? Do we have different standards for different kinds of ideas?

This controversy has returned as an argument about what is now called intelligent design. The argument has become more sophisticated. Intelligent design advocates claim that the evidence for evolution is incomplete and inconclusive and that the complexity of the universe suggests that it is the product of an intelligent designer. If others disagree, that is fine, they say. The mantra is "teach the controversy," a proposal that has been backed by President George W. Bush and Senate majority leader Bill Frist.

In Dover, Pennsylvania, the school board acted in 2004 so as to give weight to the theory of intelligent design. The board enacted two policies to accomplish this. Here are excerpts from these policies:

> Students will be made aware of gaps/problems in Darwin's theory and of other theories of evolution including, but not limited to Intelligent Design.
>
> Intelligent Design is an explanation of the Origins of Life that differs from Darwin's view. The reference book, *Of Pandas and People*, is available for students to see if they would like to explore this view in an effort to gain an understanding of what Intelligent Design actually involves. As is true with any theory, students are encouraged to keep an open mind. (Matzke, 2005)

As of this writing, eight members of the board that passed this policy have not been reelected, and the members of the new board seem disinclined to pursue the policy. A federal court has yet to rule on the matter. But whatever happens in Dover, the controversy is likely to be with us for some time. After all, the Dover board's policy is supported by very many people in the United States and appeals to the core American value of intellectual openness and fair play: "Teach the controversy. Let students decide for themselves." Isn't this the view that should be taken by schools that seek to promote the cognitive growth of their students and to create intellectual communities? To address these questions, we need to consider more deeply what we want when we want schools to be intellectual communities.

CONSTITUTIONAL ESSENTIALS

The United States is a constitutional liberal democracy. This phrase expresses three ideas that are central to our society: First, we are a liberal society. When I speak of liberalism, I have in mind a political tradition that arose in Europe largely in opposition to hierarchical forms of government, aristocracy and monarchy. (In this sense of *liberal*, both major American political parties should be viewed as such.) Its central doctrines are that human beings are to be viewed as free and equal. John Locke (1960), whose *Second Treatise on Civil Government* was, perhaps, the most formative influence on the U.S. view of government, claimed that people were free and equal by nature. The meaning of this idea is still much debated, but it is important to note that part of its meaning is fixed by what Locke intended to deny. To say that people are free and equal by nature means that no one is born with a natural right to rule or a natural right to preferential treatment. Nor is anyone a natural slave, serf, or servant. People are entitled to equal respect.

The idea that people are free by nature generally has been thought by liberals to require limits on the power of government, even democratic government. In the United States, the best example of an expression of these limits is the First Amendment to the U.S. Constitution. The First Amendment specifies that people are free to worship as they please and that they have such rights as free speech, press, and assembly. The opening phrase of the First Amendment, "Congress shall make no law . . .," indicates that these rights are viewed as limits on the power of government.

The idea that people are equal by nature and entitled to equal respect does not mean that people are in all ways the same or that they should always be treated in the same way. Instead, it means that people have equal rights before the law. In the United States, this idea is captured by the Fourteenth Amendment, which claims that people are entitled to "the equal protection of the laws."

That the United States is a democracy means primarily that political sovereignty is located in an elected legislature. Locke claimed that government rested on the consent of the governed. Lincoln described this as the government of the people, by the people, and for the people. We will discuss this more fully in Chapter 5.

To say that the United States is a constitutional liberal democracy means that the essential features of its system of government are expressed in an authoritative written document, the U.S. Constitution. There is, however, another conception of a society's constitution which is central to the ideas I want to discuss in the next three chapters. On this conception, the constitution of a society consists in those widely shared and essential understandings of what kind of society it is or wishes to be. A society's constitution is its essential character. It is its vision of political community. It is the essential answer of a political community to the question, How shall we live well together?

Constitutional essentials express a society's core values. They may be captured in a written constitution but need not be. If we think of the United States as a liberal democracy in this way, we will need to explore the meaning of notions such as freedom, equality, and democracy not as legal conceptions expressed in a body of law and through a set of institutions, but as moral ideals that should inform our interactions with other citizens.

Both ideas of a constitution are important to the work of school leaders. The written Constitution as it has been interpreted by courts and applied to schools has created a body of law with which school leaders must comply. An inquiry into constitutional essentials, however, requires leaders to form an educational conception of the norms behind the law.

Considering constitutional essentials may inform leaders with respect to such things as the following:

1. *Ideals of citizenship, character, and human relations.* School leaders cannot educate students for their role as citizens without some conception of what it means to be a citizen of a liberal democracy. Good citizens not only obey the law, vote, and participate in civic affairs, they accept certain norms of human interaction. They listen and give fair consideration to ideas with which they disagree. They respect people from different cultures. They grant freedom of conscience to those whose religions are different from their own.

2. *Ideals of the role of knowledge.* The ideals associated with free speech and a free press are not merely guarantees of the right to assert one's interests in the public arena. They are rooted in the beliefs that criticism and debate are essential to the pursuit of truth and that argument is essential to the pursuit of the common good.

3. *Ideals of organizational legitimacy.* School leaders are supposed to be fair and democratic. While school leaders are obligated to respect the sovereignty of the legislatures that have authority over public schools, the notion that leaders should be fair and democratic generally means more than that they should be conduits for legislative authority. It means that they should listen, consider the opinions of others, and create open processes for participation and deliberation. The law does not require that leaders be democratic in this way, but leaders who are not viewed as such may not be seen as fair or reasonable.

In this chapter and for much of the rest of this book, we will explore certain constitutional essentials as they apply to schools and the practice of leadership. Here the aim is not to inform the school leader about the rights and duties that are required by law. It is rather to try to understand these constitutional essentials in a way that informs educational aspirations and leadership in a society that aspires to be free, equal, and democratic. In this chapter, we will look at certain aspects of liberty that are asserted by the

First Amendment to the Constitution, intellectual liberty and freedom of religion. In the next, we consider equality. We then turn to democracy.

FREEDOM OF THOUGHT AND EXPRESSION, TRUTH, UNDERSTANDING, AND ARGUMENT

John Stuart Mill, whose views we considered in the past chapter, has written a classic defense of freedom of thought and expression entitled, *On Liberty* (1859/1956). I want to discuss the core of his argument for what he calls freedom of opinion. Mill writes,

> First, if any opinion is compelled to silence, that opinion may, for ought we can certainly know, be true. To deny this is to assume our infallibility.
>
> Second, though the silenced opinion may be an error, it may, and very often does, contain a portion of the truth; and since the general or prevailing opinion on any subject is rarely or never the whole truth, it is only by the collision of adverse opinions that the remainder of the truth has any chance of being supplied.
>
> Third, even if the received opinion be not only the truth, but the whole truth, unless it is suffered to be, and actually is rigorously and earnestly contested, it will, by most of those who receive it, be held in the manner of a prejudice, with little comprehension of its rational grounds. And not only this, but fourthly, the meaning of the doctrine itself will be in danger of being lost or enfeebled, and deprived of its virtual effect on the character and conduct; the dogma becoming a mere formal profession, inefficacious for good, but cumbering the ground and preventing the growth of any real and heartfelt conviction from reason or personal experience. (p. 64)

The first thing to notice about Mill's view is that it is a view about how truth is acquired. Truth, Mill argues, is acquired by processes that involve argument and criticism. Hence, he claims, if we seek to repress these processes in favor of our own view, we assume that we are a sufficient judge of the truth and have nothing to learn from others. In short, we assume that we are infallible.

Mill does not intend to suggest that criticism and debate are sufficient to arrive at the truth. He was an empiricist. He believed, first and foremost, that truth was discovered through experience. Nevertheless, Mill claims, criticism and debate are essential to the pursuit of truth.

Implicit in Mill's views are some assumptions about the role of public debate. In our society, freedom of expression is often viewed not so much as a tool of inquiry as a means to pursue one's interest. The many interest groups that finance our political campaigns and work hard to put their views before us are generally not much interested in open debate. They consider the views of opponents only to counter them, not to learn from them or to seek common ground. They are interested in using channels of communication to assert their own interests, not to serve the common good. Mill, however, sees debate as a means for getting at the truth and in service of the common good.

Mill's argument does not adequately note the extent to which the pursuit of truth builds on prior human achievements or the extent to which learning from experience presupposes these achievements. At the beginning of the scientific revolution, many philosophers argued that what was essential for the advancement of knowledge was careful observation of experience and the rejection of the authority of the ancients. We need to stop seeking truth in Aristotle and the Greeks and look at the world.

Modern philosophers, however, are inclined to note the extent to which the advancement of knowledge builds on prior discoveries and depends on the mastery of current concepts, organizing assumptions, and techniques of a discipline. Thomas Kuhn, whose book *The Structure of Scientific Revolutions* (1970) popularized the notion of a paradigm, is the best example. Kuhn claims that the education of a scientist begins with the mastery of the field's prevailing paradigm.

A paradigm provides the scientist with a way of seeing the world and the tools of its investigation. Most of the time, the work of science involves building on or extending the paradigm. Kuhn called this process *normal science*. Sometimes, however, when the paradigm has become dysfunctional, the task is to replace it. This is *revolutionary science*. Science, however, cannot function without paradigmatic concepts. Even when we must reject an old paradigm in favor of a new one, the evidence for the new one is, in part, the fact that it solves the problems of its predecessor. Paradigms tell scientists what the open questions are, reveal what counts as evidence and how to obtain it, and provide the lenses by which the blooming, buzzing chaos of experience is organized into object and events.

Games provide useful illustrations of this last point. Experience is not just a matter of taking in the data provided by the senses. It requires concepts to organize these data into the material of experience. Return to my earlier baseball example. Imagine that you had never heard of baseball and were taken to a game. What could you see? You might see people throwing, catching, or striking a white sphere. But you could not see home runs, strikeouts, or sacrifice bunts. People would seem to behave randomly, and the crowd's response would be puzzling. (This is the experience most Americans have watching cricket.) To *see* a game, you have to know the game's rules, grasp its essential concepts, and understand its point. Moreover, without these ideas, you could not participate in a discussion of whether good strategy required a sacrifice or hitting away, or perhaps whether it was time to put in a relief pitcher or stay with the starter.

Scientists tend to treat the prevailing paradigm in their field as authoritative much in the way that the rules of the game are authoritative for baseball. This does not mean that they view the paradigm as infallible or beyond criticism. Just as the rules of baseball can be criticized and changed for sufficient reasons, paradigms can be criticized and changed.

The point is rather that paradigms contain the ideas and techniques that are essential for thinking and arguing about scientific matters. One cannot apply or extend a paradigm that one has not mastered. Nor can one rebut it. And it is the process of rebutting a view that often provides the clue to a more adequate position. Hence, those who have not mastered the core concepts of a science, those concepts that currently are authoritative for the science, cannot function in the debates of scientists. The marketplace of scientific ideas will be closed to them. The essence of the view I am suggesting here can be put in an aphorism. We need to be willing to grant authority to some ideas without employing them in an authoritarian way.

While we should not view children altogether as so many apprentice scientists, there are some important lessons for educators here. Some ideas are provisionally authoritative, not because they were asserted by some bygone eminence or because they are revealed truths. They are authoritative because they are essential tools of thought. This needs to be clearly recognized. Mill is correct. Criticism and debate are essential to the advancement of knowledge. But knowledge is rarely advanced by the uninformed squabbling of the ignorant.

One occasionally hears a debate over the question about whether we should emphasize teaching facts or teaching how to think. This is a false dichotomy. It is not so much that thinking requires facts to think about, although it does. It is rather that thinking requires conceptual tools. Some of these tools are so obvious that we sometimes forget what marvelous achievements they are and that, despite the fact that they seem obvious to us, they were created by human beings. The alphabet is one such tool. Arithmetic and the number zero are others. We cannot get very far in chemistry without the idea of valence or in physics without inertia. Similarly, there is much we will not understand in civic education without concepts such as liberty, equality, and democracy.

These political ideas are controversial in ways in which inertia or the number zero are not. Yet they are also essential tools for understanding the constitutional essentials that organize our society. The educator must find a balance. The education provided for students must be authoritative enough and contain the right elements so that students are enabled to join in the debates and discussions that characterize the deliberative life of a free society, yet the classroom must not be closed to challenge and debate lest habits of subservience and submission be developed and the provisional character of all ideas be forgotten.

The above passage from *Tinker v. Des Moines* (1969) claims that classrooms are to be a marketplace of ideas. One justice, in a dissenting opinion, suggested that instead we should view classrooms as places where teachers teach and students learn. Neither view seems to me to be quite right. Educators surely err if they approach teaching and learning as though their task was to simply transmit some body of authoritative knowledge. This misses the importance of argument, debate, and criticism not only to the pursuit of truth but to the shaping of habits of minds. But they also err if they believe that no ideas have provisional authority.

Mill provides another kind of argument that indicates the point of argument and debate in the classroom. In his third and fourth points, he links the process of contesting an idea with maintaining its vigor. Ideas that are not contested tend to degenerate into prejudices and clichés. Eventually people lose sight not only of the reasons there are for believing them, but even of what they mean. Political "argument" provides many useful examples. Words such as *liberal* and *conservative* now seem to be used almost more as curses or honorific labels than as ideas. Often people are very sure that they are liberals or conservatives despite the fact that they would have a difficult time providing a coherent characterization of either concept.

The core of Mill's third and fourth arguments is that there is a connection between understanding the meaning of ideas and the reasons for and against them. To know what an idea means is, in part, to know what would count as evidence for or against it. If I know what "grass is green" means, I know how to identify a plant as grass, and I know what color green is. Hence, I am able to look at plants and confirm that grass is green.

Constructing hostile feelings or negative images and attaching them to ideas has just the opposite effect. The idea is given no content that permits a reasoned judgment about it. When negative images are constructed for terms such as *liberal* or *conservative*, then candidates who are successfully branded with these labels will be viewed unfavorably no matter what the merits of their views. And they will be unable to rebut these images by appealing to evidence and argument because people lack a sense of what counts for and against these positions. When this happens pervasively, a nation's politics degenerates into sloganeering, and any collective search for the truth or the common good disappears.

INDIVIDUALITY

Mill's arguments in *On Liberty* (1859/1956) are concerned not only with freedom of opinion, but also with what he calls *individuality*. In the passage quoted at the beginning of this chapter, Mill claims that there is a connection between the opportunity for free choice and individual growth. People who lack the opportunity for choice lack the need and the opportunity to develop their faculties. People who must choose their own courses of action and manage their own lives have the need and opportunity.

Mill's argument assumes two important ideas. The first is that one's cognitive capacities are brought into play largely by the need to make decisions and take action. This is the case even for the most intellectualized of problems. Solving any problem requires the selection of appropriate problem-solving tools and a determination of which, among a number of possible solutions, is the one best supported by available evidence. And if Mill's argument applies to even the academic problems that might be encountered in schools, it applies even more forcefully to the problems that must be solved by people in a society where there is the need and opportunity to lead an examined life. If people must make constant and regular choices as to how they will live their lives, then they will have the need and the opportunity to exercise those faculties that are needed to make these choices well.

A second assumption of Mill's argument is that growth requires practice. We develop those faculties and capacities we regularly employ. Here it is important that we distinguish between practice and drill or repetition. Drill is mere repetition. While drill may result in learning, such learning is likely to produce rote knowledge but is unlikely to develop complex cognitive capacities.

Practice, however, involves two additional elements. The first is a *standard* of achievement. The second is *feedback*. Consider practicing the piano. There is, of course, often an element of drill. Scales are practiced so that the fingers respond quickly and automatically. But as skill develops, practice involves a developing understanding of how the music should sound, which, in turn, permits judgments about the degree that one's current efforts meet the standards appropriate to judging a musical performance. It is this feedback on the adequacy of performance judged against standards of excellence that is key to the improvement of performance.

There is a kind of paradox at the heart of this notion of practice. The standards employed in judging practice must be authoritative and self-chosen. They must be authoritative because if they are to function as standards, they must be seen as the correct standards, the ones appropriately employed to judge performance. But they must be self-chosen because otherwise they will not be authoritative to the individual who is engaged in practicing. These comments bring us back to a conclusion that is quite similar to the one reached in discussing Mill's first argument. The development of individual capacity requires standards of achievement that carry authority over activities but are not employed in an authoritarian way.

Standards exist in the conversations and practices of communities or guilds. Ultimately, the standards of enterprises such as mathematics, music, physics, and less academic activities—such as crafts and sports—are authoritative because the communities of individuals who engage in these activities with skill and excellence recognize them as authoritative. Standards may also be contested. People will sometimes disagree about and challenge them. If the standards are to retain their authority, they must survive these challenges. Thus, the authority of any particular set of standards is always provisional and regularly tested.

Education is initiation into these various communities in which these standards are maintained. When children study mathematics, they make an acquaintance with the community of mathematicians. As they progress in mathematics, they begin to internalize and master the standards that govern the activities of mathematicians. They come to value consistency of argument and rigor of proof. They may eventually come to appreciate the kind of aesthetic appeal that mathematical ideas can have that allows them to be described as elegant or beautiful. Such standards are the constitutive norms of the community of mathematicians. Understanding them and recognizing their authority is what allows a community of mathematicians to exist. Students begin to become members of such communities as they come to understand these standards and grant their authority. If they progress far enough, they may even be able to participate in the arguments whereby such standards are challenged and revised.

Genuine freedom, the kind that involves not only possessing the formal right to choose but also the development of the capacity to choose wisely and for reasons, thus depends on the appropriation of the resources that have been developed and sustained by a variety of communities (see Strike, 1981a). Mill is right that the development of these capacities is retarded by authoritarian education and uncritical subservience to tradition, but his argument is not adequately attentive to the dependence of growth on the resources developed by other human beings and preserved in various human communities. The educator must find this balance.

Notice how Mill's arguments connect with the views of the ends of education developed in the previous chapter. There it was suggested that the core aims of education include the development of human capital, the development of the capacity for an examined life, the development of the capacity to function as a good citizen, and the development of capacities to appreciate and enjoy experience. While I resisted the characterization of these as "the life of the mind" because that term overintellectualizes the required capacities, I also suggested that these aspirations do hang together because each involves an emphasis of a kind of human development and growth to which the development of cognitive capacities is central.

Mill's arguments provide clues to what the classroom that promotes these aims must be like. Good classrooms are not places where students master mere facts; nor are they places characterized by a clash of unexamined positions. They are places that seek to provide students with the cognitive tools they will need to be good and productive citizens and to lead examined and fulfilling lives. They are also places that respect evidence and argument and that seek to connect the views that students hold or are asked to hold with a clear understanding of how these ideas are to be judged. This view provides reasons why we must respect freedom of opinion—why students must be free to discuss ideas and to argue their merits. But it also indicates that we must recognize that some ideas have provisional authority because human beings have found that they are essential tools in leading reflective lives.

LEADERSHIP AND LEARNING COMMUNITIES

Mill's (1859/1956) arguments carry relevance not only for the classroom, but for how we should understand the nature of good organizations and the authority of their leaders. In some ways, good organizations are like good classrooms. Good organizations are learning organizations. Learning organizations are task-oriented and collegial. But their essential feature is their ability to learn from research, their own experience, and their own discussions and arguments.

Learning organizations must respect and employ research. However, educational research is rarely self-applying. Often it will prove to be wrong. When it is correct, it may not apply to the unique circumstances of a particular school. Learning organizations will grant research a kind of provisional authority. However, they will also judge, interpret, and apply it through their own experience. When they work very well, they may also contribute to the research process.

The effective learning organization is one in which the leader is authoritative but not authoritarian. An essential task of the leader is to create a culture in which teachers see themselves not as autonomous rulers of their classrooms but as participants in a collective process of building and refining successful educational programs (see Westheimer, 1998). This organization explores and tests ideas collaboratively. Its members are task-oriented. They respect evidence and argument. They understand how to disagree and debate in a civil way.

As a school leader, you may lead a learning organization by establishing expectation about how the organization will function. You may also be the source of ideas. However, your ideas, like the ideas of everyone else, must be on the table for discussion, and there can be no suggestion that the leader's ideas must prevail. Leaders will need to learn how to encourage the participation of those who are tentative and refocus the manner of participation of those who are self-serving.

There is much in the culture of modern schools that makes creating such organizations difficult. Teachers may value their autonomy over their own classrooms more than a collective project of program development. School leaders may occupy roles that are in tension with these aspirations. As in our scenario, the leader may be the conduit of directives from the school district that are not open for discussion. The leader may represent management in organizations where labor management relations are stressful.

There is also much in the literature about effective leaders that can be understood in an unproductive way so far as learning organizations are concerned. Leaders are supposed to be people with visions. They are supposed to be decisive and dynamic. Leaders are supposed to be take-charge people who get things done.

These ideas are vague and platitudinous. They can be understood in appropriate ways, but they can also encourage authoritarian attitudes. Leaders who have no vision for their schools are likely to produce organizations that are drifting and directionless. At the same time, leaders who will brook no opposition for their visions are likely to become coercive and manipulative. The alternative is a style of leadership that places emphasis on creating organizations that are committed to the task of providing good education, the collegial and deliberative processes of decision making, and, above all, the rule of argument and evidence in decision making. It is your task, as a leader, to create an organization of this sort. To do so you will need to respect the views of others and to put ideas on the table for debate.

SCHOOLING AND RELIGION

On those occasions where I have had the opportunity to explore how to handle religiously sensitive issues with school leaders, I have found that it is a topic they tend to view as "the third rail" of their job: Touch it and you die. There are few topics about which Americans are more divided than how religiously sensitive issues should be treated in schools. Some Americans want prayer in schools, evolution banned, or intelligent design taught. Others insist on a high wall of separation between church and state. Some Americans see public schools as promoting a religion of secular humanism. Others believe that schools are far too open to religious influences. Americans are often fully prepared to assert their views on these matters with considerable energy, and they rarely seem interested in dialogue, compromise, or accuracy.

Given this, there is a danger that an attempt to construct a principled account of how to deal with religion in schools may produce recommendations that are hazardous to follow. Yet a principled account of how to deal with religious issues in schools is important if we are to understand how to provide a good education in a religiously diverse society.

A useful initial distinction is between activities that are, in effect, religious ceremonies, rites, or acts of worship and activities that involve dealing with religious ideas instructionally. Concerning the first, the Supreme Court has generally held that schools may not sponsor religious activities but may and sometime must permit individuals to engage in them in appropriate ways. Students may, for example, pray before a meal, but schools may not sponsor prayers. Religion may be accommodated but not promoted or endorsed.

I want to focus this discussion on the place of religion in the public school curriculum. A beginning here can be made by considering two claims about religion that are in tension:

1. *Religious ideas are ideas.* Not only that, but they are important ideas. As such, they must be considered and discussed in any adequate education, especially in one that takes the examined life seriously.

2. *Religious ideas have a special status in liberal democratic societies.* Thus, they must be treated in a special way.

Religious ideas and ideals shape people's identities. They provide direction to life. They may be a source of comfort and security. They provide pictures of the place of human beings in the cosmos. Many people believe that their religious commitments determine their eternal destiny. Many people claim that a belief in God is essential to good conduct. For many people, religious affiliations provide their primary community. Religion may determine whom one may marry, what one thinks marriage is for, whether one may divorce, and how one is to think of procreation, child rearing, and death. Religious ideas are important. This, at least, should be granted even by those who have no religious convictions.

It would seem, then, that the examination of religious ideas should be a part of any adequate education. The examination of religious ideas is clearly connected to three of the four basic ends of education I argued for in the previous chapter. It seems required by the idea of an examined life. It is also required by citizenship in a religiously pluralistic society. We cannot easily engage in a collective search for the common good without understanding the central orienting ideas of those with whom we are in dialogue. Nor can we understand our society and its history apart from understanding the religious conceptions that have shaped it. Finally, religion is, for many people, a source of meaning and enjoyment. Religion can create community and be a source of joy or peace. Religion has inspired great art and music.

All of these factors indicate that the study of religion should be a part of the education of the citizens of liberal democratic societies. Moreover, the legal obstacles to the study of religion in public schools are not as formidable as many people think. The Supreme Court has made it clear that schools may not be partisan about religion, but also that schools may engage in the secular use of sacred texts and may study religion as part of history or literature (*Abington School District v. Schempp*, 1963). Indeed, classes concerned to teach about religion are not forbidden so long as the school does not prefer one religion to another, no religious belief is required, and no religious practices are engaged in with the sponsorship of the school.

However, schools cannot go very far down the path of the study of religion without generating unsolvable problems. Some schools currently offer a course in the Bible. It remains to be seen whether such courses will be legal. Arguably, the Bible might be studied as a part of religious history or cultural literacy apart from any commitment on the part of the school to any doctrine taught therein. Certainly, when history or literature are studied, religion and religious literature should not be avoided. To do so is to distort the culture in which we live.

It is not clear, however, that courses emphasizing religion can be done either well or appropriately. The motivation of many who advocate these courses is clearly sectarian. They hope that the Bible's message will be found persuasive even if it is taught in a neutral way (and one may doubt how neutral instruction really is when no one likely to be critical is present).

What can count as neutral instruction? It is important to be clear that courses on religious matters do not become neutral because they are elective (although if there are to be such courses, it is probably wise to make them elective). What is required is that these courses be taught in such a way that no message of endorsement of religious ideas is conveyed.

Consider also that some will find that the very attempt to teach Scripture in a neutral way profanes it. And whose version of the Bible will be taught? Protestants and Catholics have a different canon. Jews reject the New Testament (as authoritative scripture) entirely. Many scholars of biblical literature argue that many of the books of the Old and New Testaments were not written by those to whom they are traditionally ascribed. For example, the Torah, generally attributed to Moses, is viewed by many scholars as a later compilation from diverse sources. So is Isaiah. How will schools deal with such views? Many religious people view such ideas as anathema. Such views, they argue, challenge the authority of sacred texts. Few religious traditionalists will wish such views taught to their children even if they are merely mentioned but not advocated.

Will these ideas be ignored? One can hardly do justice to the scholarship on biblical texts and make no mention of them. How will schools view questions of interpretation of the various doctrines taught in the Bible? Will teachers or students be able to critique what they read? How will teachers be trained? Will they be trained? Who will train them? What will they be taught? Will we develop content standards for such instruction? Who will write them, and what will they be? How will teachers test students? Such questions must be answered, but, in the American context, it is hard to see what answers will be satisfactory or acceptable.

Must we, then, ignore an area of life that many find important because it is also so controversial? Before I make some suggestions about this, we need also to consider why religious ideas have special status in liberal democratic societies. The First Amendment of the U.S. Constitution seems to treat religion differently from freedom of speech, press, and assembly. Freedom of speech, press, and assembly are valued largely in that they enable participation in a marketplace of ideas. A marketplace of ideas is seen as essential to a viable democracy. The common good must be sought through vigorous debate. The First Amendment, however, does not envision a marketplace of religious ideas. Its main purpose is to secure the right to worship in freedom with those of one's choice. Its intent is to secure a right to be exercised privately in association with the like-minded. It is not to facilitate public debate of religious ideas. The First Amendment tends to see free speech as protected because it serves public purposes, but it privatizes religion.

Our society rests on the assumption that shared religious commitments cannot be the basis of our political community and that religious ideas cannot be the basis of public policy. This view of the role of religion has strong roots in the religious wars that followed the Protestant Reformation. If people believe that a political community must be rooted in a shared religion, they may have civil peace so long as they are agreed on what that shared religion is. If, however, there are competing faiths and it is thought that the political community must be rooted in one of them, we have a formula for endless civil strife and sectarian violence. Our Constitution privatizes religion to reduce sectarian strife.

There is a second essential goal of the religion clauses of the First Amendment. This is the desire to protect freedom of conscience. The need to protect freedom of conscience results from the unique role that religious belief can play in people's lives. People often experience religious prescriptions as commands that must be obeyed. Hence, when religious commands are at odds with the requirements of the state, they may reply, "I must obey God rather than man." Also, religion is often central to people's identity. It not only tells them what they must do, it tells them who they are. It is central to their being. Finally, religion is orienting to people. It locates them in the cosmos, gives meaning to life, and provides purpose.

Societies that wish to respect freedom of conscience and avoid sectarian strife must give religious ideas a distinct status. While they may recognize that our religious traditions have shaped public values and legal conceptions, and while they may value the many contributions people of faith make to the common good, they cannot grant any distinctive set of religious ideas provisional authority in public affairs. To do so is to declare that those who do not ascribe to these ideas are second-class citizens. It is to put their freedom of conscience at risk, to erode their allegiance to the political order, and to invite civil strife.

Apparently, more than a third of American citizens would support an amendment to the Constitution declaring the United States to be a Christian nation. Christianity has, of course, had a profound influence on the culture of the United States and most of the Western world. But the United States is not a Christian nation in at least two important ways. First, there are millions of U.S. citizens who are not Christians. There are Jews, Muslims, Hindus, Buddhists, Wiccans, atheists, and agnostics in large numbers. Second, the U.S. Constitution is committed to the notion that, so far as our political culture is concerned, we are a secular society. Here *secular* does not mean religiously antagonistic. It means religiously neutral.

Consider what it would mean for many Americans were the Constitution to declare that the United States was a Christian nation. Even if this declaration were a mere platitude, it demeans the status of those among us who are not Christians. It suggests that although they are citizens, they exist here on the suffrage of the Christian majority, and it suggests that their convictions carry no weight in public affairs while those of Christians do.

Moreover, any declaration that distinctly Christian ideas carry weight in public affairs threatens the freedom of conscience of Christians as well as non-Christians. Christians do not, after all, agree either about a wide range of doctrines or about the implications of these doctrines for law and policy. Once we take the view that religious doctrines have relevance for policy, the government will need to develop views as to which interpretations of these doctrines are true and what implications they have for policy. The government, thus, inevitably will begin to take sides in religious controversies and give some doctrines official support and others not.

That the preferred doctrines are to be Christian doctrines will not prevent governments from deciding disputes among Christians and thus from preferring one sect to another. Not even Christians will be free in a Christian nation! We should recall that the wars of religion that caused so much death and misery a few centuries ago were wars between Christian sects.

What does it mean for the state to be neutral concerning religion? At the most general level, it means that the state cannot act so as to either advance or to inhibit religion. This idea of neutrality needs to be understood as concerned with intent, not effect. Any quality educational program may have an effect on some religion. If schools create classrooms where ideas are seriously debated and discussed, some religions may find that they are unable to compete in the marketplace of ideas.

Schools are not required to refrain from expressing any message that is found to be inconsistent with or inimical to some religion. If this were required, it is difficult to see how we would have a curriculum at all, let alone one that was genuinely educative. What is required of schools is to not engage in programs and activities that are intended to benefit or disadvantage some religion.

Intent has to do with the justification of practices. If a school puts up a crèche at Christmas, this is not excused because the person who put it up did not actually think of its association with Christianity. The question is, Can this be justified in a way that does not presuppose an intent to benefit one religion over others or over no religion? The singing of Christmas music might have a neutral justification if it was part of an attempt to familiarize students with various religious and cultural expressions. The crucial question is whether an educational activity can be coherently justified in neutral and secular terms.

If we are to include religion in the curriculum in a responsible way, we must include it in a way that avoids advocacy or endorsement. This means that when religious ideas are discussed in the curriculum, they may not be taught as though they carry authority. In a physics class, the ideas that are expressed in the text have the kind of provisional authority that I have argued is essential to learning. They have this kind of authority because they are viewed by the community of physicists as essential for doing physics and because they have survived the arguments and tests to which they have been put by members of this community. We could not teach physics without treating the concept of inertia as authoritative. In public institutions, religious ideas cannot carry such authority. To grant religious ideas this form of authority is to invite civil strife and threaten the freedom of conscience of those who dissent.

EVOLUTION, CREATIONISM, AND INTELLIGENT DESIGN

Let us return to the question of teaching evolution and creationism/intelligent design. Why would it be objectionable to give creationism or intelligent design equal status with evolution in the classroom?

The kind of creationism we are talking about here is not the proposition that there is a God whose creative activity is expressed in the universe. This view does not claim to be a scientific account of origins, nor is it in competition with any scientific accounts about origins. It is entirely metaphysical. It asserts no explanatory hypotheses and makes no empirical claims.

The creationism we are discussing claims to be a scientific theory that accounts for observed phenomena and is supported by empirical evidence. This claim was central to the scientific creationism of the Louisiana statute, but it applies with equal force to the more recent repackaging of creationism that emphasizes the claim that the complexity of the universe requires a belief in intelligent design. Since many people in our society believe this, why should we not give this view credence in the science classroom and provide it equal time with evolution?

The first thing to note about the Louisiana statute that proposed equal time for creationism is that while it claimed to promote the academic freedom of students by providing them the evidence for two competing theories, it did not seek to create a marketplace of ideas. In fact, the messages about creationism that teachers were to provide to students were highly scripted, and open discussion of the merits of the two views was not encouraged.

Similarly, it is not clear that those who advocate intelligent design seek to create a marketplace of ideas. They seem to wish to require teachers to tell their students that evolution is not proven and that there are problems with it. But there is no invitation to put the arguments for these claims on the table and to discuss them in the classroom. Indeed, one suspects that advocates of intelligent design would not welcome such a discussion because they would not trust biology teachers to take their views seriously. For advocates of creationism and intelligent design, "teach the controversy" does not appear to mean "debate the views in the classroom."

An important point here is that the idea of academic freedom is intended to do more than protect free and open debate. It is intended to protect scholars from political influence of a sort that seeks to determine truth by political processes.. Truth is not determined by majority rule. It is determined by reasoned argument. The import of the Louisianan statute is not so much to permit students to make up their minds. It is to claim that creationism is viewed as a viable hypothesis by the scientific community. Since it is not, this amounts to a state-mandated lie.

A useful way to view the import of the Louisiana statute and the advocacy of intelligent design is that what they demand is that schools agree to treat two competing theories of origins as equally authoritative. Treating competing paradigms as equally authoritative is not inherently problematic. Areas such as philosophy, psychology, or literary interpretation do not have one set of paradigmatic ideas that are viewed as uniquely authoritative. Instead, they recognize the authority of a set of competing paradigms, and these competing paradigms are collectively authoritative for those who wish to engage in the work of the field. This, I believe, is the best understanding of what advocates of creationism and intelligent design want. They want schools to recognize, as a matter of policy, that there are two views that are authoritative for the study of origins.

There are three reasons why we should not accept this view. The first is that while evolution is universally viewed by biologists as authoritative for work in biology—one cannot think like a biologist without employing the concepts of evolutionary theory—it is simply not true that creationism or intelligent design are viewed as viable alternatives to evolution within any of the sciences to which it is relevant. Creationism impacts not just biology but geology, paleontology, and cosmology. Evolutionary theory carries authority in all of these; creationism in none.

The second reason is that there is no science of creationism or of intelligent design. Such science as there is consists of arguments against evolution. It is said that there are gaps in the fossil record and that life is too complex to have evolved. These arguments look for gaps in our knowledge and put God into these gaps. But beyond the claim that "God did it," there are no hypotheses proposed and no investigations suggested. There is no positive program of investigation that is warranted by these views—only a rebuttal of evolution and a God of the gaps. Creationism and intelligent design cannot be authoritative for the investigation of origins because they do not function to guide investigation into the phenomena with which they are concerned. There is no paradigm to be coequal with evolution.

The third reason is that creationism and intelligent design are religious ideas, not scientific ones. Their content is religious, and it is believed for reasons of theology and faith, not reasons of science. And creationism and intelligent design are partisan religious ideas. Many versions of Christianity, Judaism, and other faiths have come to terms with evolution. Some have even given it theological import. And, of course, there are religions with very different creation stories. Hence, for schools to give creationism or intelligent design the kind of authority in the biology classroom that is demanded by the equal status view is not only to give authority to a religious view in the classroom, but to take sides in a disagreement among religions.

Notwithstanding the above comments, educators must respect the freedom of conscience of creationist students. When I was a high school student, my biology teacher began the unit on evolution by saying something like this: "I know that some of you will not accept evolution because of your religious convictions. I will respect your religious convictions in that I will not ask that you *agree* with evolution or expect you to affirm any convictions on the topic. However, you should also know that evolution is central to modern biology. I cannot teach biology conscientiously and not teach evolution. Hence, I will teach it and expect you to know what I teach. I will be careful to phrase any exam questions on the topic so that you can answer them without expressing a view as to whether you believe in evolution."

This, I think, is the right response. The freedom of conscience of creationist students must be respected. This does not require that they be exempted from any study of evolution, but it does preclude public schools from requiring them to affirm a belief (see Macedo, 1995; *West Virginia State Board of Education v. Barnette*, 1943).

How shall we deal with religion in the curriculum? I do not think it wise for educators to attempt to create a marketplace of ideas in their classrooms where religious conceptions are examined and critiqued. Not only is this likely to become a third rail, it is likely to violate the conscience of many students. It is simply not the kind of thing that public schools are able to do well.

At the same time, religious ideas are ideas. They can be debated and appraised, and it is important that students be able to do so. We should not pretend that religious ideas do not exist or are unimportant to our students. Schools should not create the illusion that we live in a religion-free world. Nor should we give in to the modern prejudice that all religions are equally true. After all, religious claims frequently contradict one another. Given this, it is a matter of elementary logic that some of them must be false. Moreover, the pretense that all religions are equally true itself offends the convictions of those who believe their religion to be uniquely true.

The best advice I can give is that educators should deal with religious ideas where and when they naturally occur in subject areas such as history, literature, and music. I do not think it wise to attempt to treat religion or the Bible as separate topics or distinct subjects. To be sure, religious ideas are ideas. There is an educational point to discussing them. Doing so is part of living an examined life. Doing so well without inviting sectarian strife and violating the conscience of many is impossible in the majority of American schools at the current time.

CONCLUSIONS

This chapter has argued two central ideas. First, inquiry, discussion, and debate should characterize the classroom. Educators have recently come to argue that American schools should be characterized by what is called *academic press*. The idea is to recognize that academic achievement is the central purpose of schooling and that schools should set high expectations for achievement. So they should. At the same time, no conception of academic press that does not include a central place for the debate of important ideas is worthy of American democracy.

It is ideas, vigorously tested and contested, that are central to the goals of a good education. However, the classroom must also recognize the authority of those ideas that function as the tools of thought and inquiry in various domains and that are essential if free and open debate is to be a means for the pursuit of truth rather than a babble of self-assertion. It is these intellectual tools that should be central in what we expect our children to know.

Second, while religious ideas are ideas, they should be distinguished from other ideas because free societies whose members come from diverse religious traditions can avoid violations of conscience and sectarian strife only by insisting that public institutions be religiously neutral. This means that public schools may not endorse religious ideas, and it means that while public schools may discuss religion in areas such as history or literature, they may not give religious ideas authority in the classroom.

Recall again the location of these views in the larger argument of this book. School leaders are expected to be accountable. Often this accountability is expressed via officially recognized content standards and tests where mastery of academic content is measured. While content standards and tests may define and measure important content, they do not add up to a conception of a good education, and they may be pursued in miseducative ways. Hence, you, as a school leader, need to ensure that teaching and learning are in the service of a reasonable conception of education. The best way to do this is to create a learning organization in your school wherein a praiseworthy vision of education is debated and prized.

4

Constitutional Essentials, Part II

Equal Opportunity and Multicultural Community

No state shall. . . . deny to any person within its jurisdiction the equal protection of the laws.

—Equal Protection clause of the Fourteenth
Amendment to the U.S. Constitution

Segregation of white and colored children in public schools has a detrimental effect upon the colored children. The impact is greater when it has the sanction of the law; for the policy of separating the races is usually interpreted as denoting the inferiority of the negro group. A sense of inferiority affects the motivation of a child to learn. Segregation with the sanction of law, therefore, has a tendency to [retard] the education and mental development of negro children and to deprive them of some of the benefits they would receive in a racially integrated school system. . . . We conclude that in the field of public education the doctrine of "separate but equal" has no place. Separate educational facilities are inherently unequal.

—*Brown v. Board of Education* (1954)

Effects of inputs have come to constitute the basis for assessment of school quality (and thus equality of opportunity).

—James Coleman (1968, p. 211)

What would equality of opportunity look like . . . ? One might argue that it should show a convergence so that even though two population groups begin school with different levels of skill on the average, the average of the group that begins lower moves up to coincide with that of the group that begins higher.

—James Coleman (1968, p. 212)

PROLOGUE AND SCENARIO

One of the constitutional essentials of a liberal democracy is equality. In this chapter, I explore how equality applies to schooling. I argue three essential points: First, I argue that equal opportunity should be viewed as a theory of fair competition in which children have a fair chance to succeed that does not depend on background characteristics such as race, ethnicity, gender, or socioeconomic status. Second, I discuss the ethics of resource allocation, emphasizing how we should treat high-needs students. I argue that we should approach resource allocation with a sense that each student should be entitled to the resources required to enable that child to achieve a set of capacities that are within his or her reach and that facilitate a life of dignity within a community. Third, I suggest that we need to create educational communities characterized by a sense that we are all in it together. I argue that such communities enable a number of educational goals, including the development of good citizens and the pursuit of the examined life. This also generates an appropriate conception of multiculturalism and makes it easier to achieve equal opportunity.

To focus the discussion of these matters a bit, let us return to our initial scenario and expand one part of it.

The parents and teachers in your school have taken considerable pride in the success of its program. And they are unhappy that the school board in the district has imposed a number of requirements on your school that will modify this program. Yet it is not true that your program succeeds for everyone. A careful look at your program reveals several things.

First, in your school, as in most American schools, poor and minority students do not do as well as those students from white and affluent families. While it is true that these students do better than their counterparts in other schools in your district, there is nevertheless a quite noticeable achievement gap. Are you responsible to remedy these gaps? How will you do this?

Second, like most American schools, your school has a significant number of children with various disabilities, ranging from deafness and Down syndrome to hyperactivity and autism. These students all have the required Individualized Education Programs (IEPs). Most of them function in the regular classroom and receive various additional services as appropriate. At the same time, for many of these students, there is more that could be done. The trouble is that this "more" is often costly. Your school district has become quite concerned about the rapidly rising costs of special education. They are pressing you and the other principals in your district to contain these costs. So there are real restraints on your ability to provide additional services.

One particular case has caught your attention and has come to represent the issue to you. Carli is mildly autistic. She is in the first grade and is clearly struggling. Her IEP specifies that she is to participate in a pull-out program with a special resource teacher who comes to your school twice a week to work with Carli and several other children. Carli's parents are pressing you to expand this program.

They argue that before Carli began attending your school, she was enrolled in an intensive preschool program for autistic children. She had made considerable progress in this program, but it is very expensive and her parents were unable to afford to continue Carli in it. They had also failed in their attempt to get your school district to pay the tuition for Carli to attend this school. Now they are pressing you to expand the role of the resource teacher. They argue that this teacher is helpful to Carli, but that Carli does not have enough time with her. They also argue that the progress that Carli made in her previous school is disappearing and that Carli is not doing well in your school.

You agree and have asked your district to make the resource teacher available more often for Carli and other students. The district is, in fact, willing. But they have made it clear to you that you must find the dollars for this additional time in your own budget. This means that something else will have to go. And it may mean that you will have to trade Carli's welfare for the welfare of some other children. There is no loose money lying about. Should you do this? And how will you decide how to balance Carli's needs against the needs of other children?

A final matter has caught your attention. Your teachers have done a good job in helping your students to understand how important academic achievement is. Often the appeal has been to the argument that doing well in school is crucial to getting into college and getting a good job. This is a message that is reinforced by many parents at home. But this seems to you to have had one unfortunate consequence. Your students seem to feel that they are in competition with one another for grades. While you want your students to have high aspirations for themselves, it is too bad that even some of your fourth graders seem to be stressed about whether they will get into Harvard.

You have tried to introduce a bit of cooperative learning in your school. Some of the more academically talented children have resisted this, and you have had a few complaints from parents who argue that the progress of their children is being held back by their less-talented peers.

There is another problem that distresses you even more. You have noted that children resist having some of their peers who have IEPs and who are viewed as less likely to contribute to their group's work as a part of their cooperative learning groups. There have been a few unkind words and hurt feelings. Unfortunately, some of these words and hurt feelings have had racial overtones. You want your students to experience their classroom and your school as a community. Is this a worthwhile aspiration? What does it mean? And how does it relate to the diversity in your school and to your desire to provide equal opportunity?

Let's begin to discuss these issues with some background on equality.

BROWN V. BOARD OF EDUCATION AND ITS AFTERMATH

In 1954, *Brown v. Board of Education* overturned the "separate but equal doctrine" of *Plessy v. Ferguson* (1896). The passage quoted above from *Brown* seems to claim that segregation is illegal because it has negative consequences for the achievement of black students. Indeed, it seems to announce a causal theory to account for the black/white achievement gap. That theory claims that segregation stigmatizes black children, leading to low self-esteem. Low self-esteem, in turn, has a negative effect on achievement. Hence, the reason that separate schools cannot be equal is that the segregated environment itself, apart from other school resources and characteristics, has consequences for achievement.

Some legal scholars have suggested that this is a misinterpretation of *Brown* (see Strike, 1981b). The rights of minority students should not depend on speculative empirical theories about self-esteem and achievement. Instead, they claim, the fundamental point of *Brown* rests on the essential commitment that underlies the Fourteenth Amendment, a commitment to the equal dignity, equal worth, and equal rights of all citizens. The point of *Brown* is to note that segregation rests on a presumption that black children are unworthy to associate with white children. This presumption cannot be reconciled with the equality of all citizens that is the essential presumption of the Fourteenth Amendment. If so, *Brown* is more about equal dignity than equal outcomes. It appeals more to the principle of equal respect than to benefit maximization.

The Supreme Court, after several painful and inconclusive decades of attempting to desegregate American public schools, has interpreted the

Fourteenth Amendment to prohibit de jure but not de facto segregation. It has defined de jure segregation as a racial imbalance between schools caused by intentional state action (see *Keyes v. School District No. 1*, 1973). This definition has broadened and narrowed the idea of illegal segregation. A school district may be illegally segregated even if it does not have and has never had laws requiring the separation of the races. Drawing attendance zones to create racial imbalance is de jure segregation. However, racial imbalance that results from a neighborhood school policy and residential segregation is not de jure segregation and is, therefore, not illegal, even if it results in significant racial imbalance between schools.

The Court in *Board of Education of Oklahoma City v. Dowell* (1991) has also allowed districts that were under desegregation orders and deemed to have complied with these orders for a suitable period of time to return to neighborhood schools even if the result is a significant increase in schools that are largely one-race schools. Because many urban areas have large concentrations of minority students and considerable residential segregation, these decisions have resulted in considerable de facto segregation in schooling.

Why is this important? First, it means that desegregated schools need not be integrated schools. And in many areas, they are not. Poor black students often experience considerable racial isolation in education. Second, it suggests that Americans (collectively) no longer seem to view integration as a means to the improvement of minority education, or, if they do, they lack the political will to create integrated schools.

Is integration a means to improve minority achievement? We should remember that when *Brown* was decided, black Americans tended to achieve at significantly lower rates than white Americans. While this achievement gap has narrowed somewhat, much of it remains. Does integration affect these achievement gaps?

Theories that suggest that integration might benefit minority achievement often depend on the idea that social class has a significant effect on what children learn in school. This claim about social class is both about individuals and about the composition of the school. There is much research to suggest that a child's social class is a significant predictor of his or her achievement and that the socioeconomic composition of a school itself affects the achievement of its students. The classical formulation of this view is that of James Coleman (1968), who is quoted above.

Whom one goes to school with is important. Minority status is not perfectly or inevitably associated with social class, but it is strongly associated. Minority students are far more likely to come from poor families than are white students. Hence, for several decades after *Brown*, many policy makers viewed school integration as a tool for improving minority achievement largely because racial desegregation tended to produce some degree of socioeconomic integration. There was, of course, much debate about all this, but regardless of the truth of the matter, U.S. federal courts are unlikely, in the near future, to view desegregation as a means toward significant school integration or advancing minority achievement.

We should consider these facts in the light of other trends. One is population migration. Since World War II, there has been a significant migration of poor minority populations into urban areas and of white and middle-class populations into suburbs. This has been accompanied by an out-migration of economic resources to the suburbs. Finally, while it is difficult to characterize trends in school finance, it seems generally the case that in urban areas, where the need for educational resources is greater, resources are scarcer. Thus, at the beginning of the twenty-first century, American schools are characterized by a situation where schools are significantly segregated by race and class and where schools with the most need have the fewest resources. The social will to alter these facts seems weak. If equal opportunity is to be provided by schools, it must be provided under these circumstances.

There are other concerns about racial integration that must be considered in working toward just educational policies. One such concern is citizenship. Good citizens must view one another as equals and of equal worth. This goes beyond mere tolerance (if tolerance conveys an attitude of putting up with or taking a live-and-let-live attitude). It requires that citizens respect one another, one another's choices, and one another's cultures. It also requires that citizens be able to engage one another in dialogue in pursuit of the common good.

If students are to achieve these attitudes toward one another, they must engage one another. Schools with diverse populations seem excellent places for students from diverse backgrounds to form these attitudes and develop these understandings and skills. Of course, we should not assume that this will happen merely because a school or a classroom places diverse students in a common space. Productive interactions must be planned and provided for. Such interactions are, of course, difficult where schools are segregated.

EQUAL OPPORTUNITY

In the discussion of *Brown,* I suggested two important points. The first is that *Brown* is more about equal citizenship than equal opportunity. That is, while *Brown* does point to the educational harm that segregation does to black children, its central message, as interpreted by later decisions, is one of equal citizenship and equal rights. People are not regarded as equal citizens when they are compelled by law to lead separate lives. Second, I suggested that the way in which the law of desegregation has worked out in connection with other trends in population dynamics and school finance has not made the educator's task of providing for equality of opportunity any easier. These various social dynamics have tended to concentrate poor and minority students in urban areas where educational need is greater and resources are fewer.

This second point assumes a view about what equal opportunity is. Equal opportunity requires more than nondiscriminatory access to a free public education. Arguably, if all we mean by equal opportunity is that race is no longer employed to assign or deny educational benefits, we have come close to achieving that. But what is wanted is schools that produce equal results.

Your school appears to be doing well but is not producing equal results. You are right to be concerned that there is a failure of justice involved. Why? Consider that one of the noteworthy features of *NCLB* is that it requires achievement data to be disaggregated so that progress can be tracked for different groups, and it requires progress for each group. Not only that, but it requires that achievement gaps between different groups be closed. Why?

A simple explanation is that *NCLB* is interested in two distinct goals. The first is higher achievement. The second is equal opportunity. As the earlier quotes from James Coleman suggest, both can be gauged by looking at achievement. This seems quite plausible in the case of the assessment of school quality. Good schools are those that produce good results. We might quibble about how we should measure what results, but it would certainly be a strange world if we considered a school to be a good one because we spent a lot of money on it, had teachers with good credentials, and had fine libraries and excellent equipment, but no one learned very much.

It might, however, seem more plausible to think of equal opportunity in terms of the equality of inputs. One reason concerns the word *opportunity*. It seems to suggest that we are interested in making sure that every student has the same chance to learn rather than that every student learn the same amount or the same thing. We might go on to argue that there should be a division of labor between the school and the student. The school provides the opportunity, but students must make the effort to take advantage of this opportunity. It may be the fault of the school when one student learns less than another if the school provided that student an inferior educational experience; however, it may also be that one student worked harder than another, had different interests, or had different abilities. In cases such as these, the fact that the same inputs produce different outputs is no fault of the school and no failure of equal opportunity.

Another factor suggesting this conclusion is that many of the battles over equal opportunity seem to have been battles over inputs. Much of the litigation about school finance (see *San Antonio Independent School District v. Rodriguez*, 1973) has argued that it is unfair that schools are financed by property taxes with the result that children who live in different tax jurisdictions have unequally financed schools. These suits have aimed (with modest, but limited, success) to equalize expenditures among districts with different wealth bases.

I want to show you why Coleman and *NCLB* are correct. We can assess the quality of schools by looking at achievement, and we can assess whether we have achieved equal opportunity by looking at achievement. Of course it does not follow that this is easy to do or that every law or policy that mandates such assessments is wise. Nevertheless, the project of judging school quality and equality by the effects of schooling rather than inputs into schooling is an important one.

One of the features of a just society is that its economic positions are available on a nondiscriminatory basis. Hiring, for example, should be based solely on criteria relevant to the work to be done. People should be hired on the basis of their ability to do the work for which they are hired. Positions should be open to talents (Rawls, 1971). But this is not sufficient.

Imagine a society which systematically hired the most qualified people to do the work available but which failed to provide the opportunity to acquire a talent on an equal basis. Perhaps some students were unable to acquire a talent because they came from poor families or were members of a disfavored racial or ethnic minority and the educational opportunities available to them were systematically inferior to the opportunities available to others. Such a society might claim to have fair hiring, but this claim to justice would be hollow because some people would be able to acquire the qualifications required to be hired and others not. Such a society would be unjust because it lacked equal opportunity. If we presume that educational institutions are among the primary places in which relevant qualifications are acquired, then the society is unjust because it lacks equality of educational opportunity.

This view of equal educational opportunity views it as part of a theory of fair competition. It assumes that employment opportunities and other valued social positions are competitive and justly allocated on the basis of the possession of relevant qualifications so long as the opportunity to acquire these qualifications is fair. A common metaphor: Life is a race. It is okay if the race is to the swift. But it is not okay if the track on which people compete is unequal, that is, if only some must run through the mud or face hurdles. Equal educational opportunity attempts to create a fair race, a level playing field.

How can we cash out this metaphor? The metaphor assumes that it is fair if some factors affect outcomes, but not others. But what factors permissibly affect achievement, and what factors ought not to affect achievement? Here is what seems to be a plausible intuitive list, one that is implicit in the previous discussion: Achievement may permissibly be affected by ability, effort, or aspirations. There is no unfairness if those who are more able do better. There is no unfairness if those who work harder do better. And there is no unfairness if achievement is affected by personal choices.

There is, of course, more to be said about these factors. Choice, for example, should not be coerced or manipulated. If the educational choices of some minorities are made in the reasonable anticipation of job market discrimination, these choices cannot justify unequal outcomes. There are thus complexities lurking in the details of this list; nevertheless, ability, effort, and choice have intuitive plausibility in our culture as factors that permissibly influence outcomes.

Here are some of the factors that should not affect achievement: race, ethnicity, family wealth, religion, gender, or sexual preference. Here, too, there may be complexities. Suppose choice is influenced by religion. We might think it suspicious, for example, if disproportionately more Catholics than Protestants graduate from college, but we should not have the same reaction if fewer Amish graduate. They do not wish to go to college. Suppose we call those characteristics that permissibly affect achievement *morally appropriate* characteristics, meaning that they may have a legitimate connection with achievement. We can then call those characteristics that should not connect with achievement *morally inappropriate* characteristics.

Next, we need a picture of what we hope schools will do in creating equal opportunity. The discussion so far suggests that what we hope schools will do is to break or at least weaken the link between morally inappropriate characteristics and school achievement and, eventually, life prospects. Suppose we picture the desired relationships as seen below.

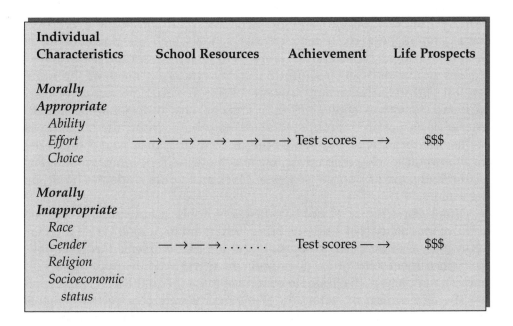

In this diagram, the arrows represent causality. When the arrows are replaced by dots, that indicates that causality is disrupted.

The model assumes that background characteristics interact with school resources so as to produce achievement. We should understand a school resource as anything about a school that has a significant effect on achievement. It might include money, teacher quality, the nature or quality of instruction, or the characteristics of other students. The model views test scores as a measure of achievement. It is worth noting again that test scores are a measure of but not the meaning of achievement. Tests may be more or less accurate and more or less complete indices of what we want schools to accomplish. For example, they are more likely to be adequate measures of whether students can read than they are of whether they have become good citizens.

The model also assumes that one reason why we value achievement is that it has a significant impact on life prospects. The effect of achievement on life prospects is often studied by employing income as the measure of life success. Here, too, the model assumes that income is a relevant measure of life success, not the full meaning of it. Other things may count; indeed, they may be more important. Income is employed because it can be measured more readily than job satisfaction or friendship.

What the model (which is normative, not descriptive) is intended to display is that schools should employ their resources in such a way that the causal effects of morally inappropriate characteristics, such as race or socioeconomic status on achievement, are reduced or eliminated, and achievement is solely the product of the interaction of morally appropriate characteristics and school resources. Ideally, the correlation between morally irrelevant background characteristics and socially relevant outcomes should be zero. It may be that schools lack the power to fully achieve this ideal. Nevertheless, it is this to which we should aspire.

The model does not require that every student achieve at the same level. It permits achievement to vary insofar as variations are associated with such factors as ability, effort, or choice. What it does require is that, insofar as is possible, groups of students whose group membership is defined by race, gender, or some other morally inappropriate characteristic achieve at levels comparable to the achievement of other groups. For example, the distribution of scores of black and white students should be the same.

Equal opportunity is not satisfied if schools simply pass along the kinds of inequality that students bring with them to school. While it is certainly a good thing when schools do nothing that worsens these inequalities (since inequality often does seem to worsen while students are in school), the point is to eliminate or reduce these inequalities.

The elimination or reduction of inequality may require that schools allocate more resources to those students who come to school behind because they belong to a disfavored group. This may seem to some to be favoritism or even reverse discrimination. It is not. The point of schools so far as equal opportunity is concerned is to mitigate the inheritance of inequality across generations—to give each child a fair chance to succeed, regardless of the social position of his or her parents or community. When children's social location prior to or outside of school has a negative impact on their ability to learn, it is the point of schools to take that into account and to help such disadvantaged students achieve parity with their more favored peers.

This last point requires more comment. One of the more popular slogans of the day is the claim that "all children can learn." No doubt the phrase is true in some sense, but what does it mean? One meaning that we should embrace is that educators may not conclude that children who are from disfavored groups or backgrounds are unable to learn and to respond to this condition by lack of effort or by employing the alleged disabilities of these children as an excuse for poor performance (the child's or the school's).

There is a second meaning that we should resist. This is that disadvantaged backgrounds (characterized, perhaps, by poverty or discrimination) have no effect on the capacity of children to profit from schooling. We know this to be false! Indeed, it is quite likely that the cumulative effects of poverty and discrimination on achievement are beyond the capacity of schooling, even good schooling, to fully ameliorate apart from the combined efforts of other social institutions (see Rothstein, 2004).

Disadvantaged students often have unstable housing and change schools frequently, tend to have poorer health and nutrition, and are read to and talked to by adults at much lower rates than are middle-class students. These and other aspects of social class have an effect on the capacity of children to learn, and it does not benefit them to deny the reality of these facts or to pretend that schools can fully ameliorate their educational consequence when they cannot. Indeed, it sets up schools for failure. (What are we going to say in 2014 [the target date of *NCLB*] if all children are not proficient and achievement gaps remain?)

What is important is how you respond to these external inequalities. It does not follow from what I have said that schools are altogether ineffective in ameliorating the effects of poverty or discrimination or that educators are exempt from doing their best to do so. Hence, educators have a duty to do the best that they can do to ameliorate the effects of social class on student achievement. Educators should also consider the importance of providing support for other kinds of social reforms that might help break the link between discrimination, poverty, and achievement.

The limits of the model should be noted. It is not a model of a good education, merely an equal one. We might make education more equal by making it equally bad for everyone or by neglecting the education of higher achieving groups. We may also create the illusion of equality by setting low standards that almost everyone meets. (A danger *NCLB* invites.) Or we may employ measures of achievement on which higher achieving students "top out" so that when lower achieving students do better, achievement gaps appear to be reduced.

Moreover, the model focuses on inequality between different groups. It does not address inequality *within* groups. For example, one can imagine schools in which the distribution of test scores of black and white students is the same, but where the difference between high- and low-performing black and white students is large. While such schools might claim to have created equality of opportunity, they seem, nevertheless, unequal in some other sense.

Because educators are now under enormous pressure to increase test scores and equalize results among different groups, it is important to again emphasize the notion that test scores are a measure of achievement, not the meaning of it. Tests may imperfectly measure what they aim to measure, and they do not attempt to measure all that is of value in a good education.

Educators who teach disadvantaged children may be under more than average pressure to raise test scores and, hence, under more than average pressure to reduce the curriculum to what is tested for. Hence, there is danger that attempts to reduce measured inequality may increase inequalities in that which is not measured.

It is one thing to align your curriculum to a set of standards and tests, and quite another to altogether surrender your judgment as an educator to them. Tests must be used responsibly. To do so, you need a reasonable conception of the meaning of a good education, and this conception should take into account the needs of the population being taught. You also need the courage to resist such temptation as exists to engage in such vices as teaching to the test and program distortion.

Equal opportunity is not provided by an education that equalizes the tested performance of disadvantaged or disfavored students if the means for achieving that is teaching to the test or programmatic distortion. In both cases, the measured results will be an inaccurate measure of equal opportunity because they fail to measure all that is relevant or measure all that is relevant adequately. Students do not receive an equal education if the education they receive is less rich or varied than that available to others merely because they test well.

I am not arguing that educators may not respond to students who bring deficiencies with them to school or who are behind in basic skills with a program that emphasizes remediation of these deficiencies. If a student is behind in reading, it may well be a good thing if that student's program trades some art or music for more reading instruction. I am arguing that educators need to make reflective judgments about such things so that the program that students receive is determined by their needs rather than by the needs of educators to produce higher scores.

JUSTICE AND RESOURCE ALLOCATION

School leaders face other issues of justice and fairness in addition to equality of educational opportunity. Students compete for scarce resources. I do not mean that they compete directly, each pressing his or her case. Nevertheless, resources are scarce, and sometimes decisions have to be made to support some programs and not others. Not all needs can be met, and we cannot satisfy all of the demands for resources pressed on us even when the needs that might be met are quite real. How do we decide between alternative demands for resources? How do we decide, for example, whether to provide additional resources to Carli if we must do so by taking them from programs that benefit other students?

Sometimes decisions about resource allocation can be made on the basis of judgments about program quality. We choose this program or allocation of resources rather than that one because this program, this allocation of resources, is more effective. We have enough money for a new teacher. We want to emphasize improvement in reading. Shall we use the money to hire a new teacher and reduce class size, or shall we hire a reading specialist? The issue is largely one of effectiveness.

Sometimes we can make decisions about resource allocation on the basis of our objectives. Different programs serve different objectives. Which objectives are more important? Which important objectives are currently not adequately met and could be better served by additional resources?

Asking about the nature of our objectives and the effectiveness of our means are essential to any reasonable process of decision making. Hence, they are essential to thinking about resource allocation. They do not, however, provide a simple metric. Perhaps we believe that mathematics is more important than music. But music may help engage students in school and lead to better performance in math.

Objectives are often difficult to compare, and we are often woefully ignorant about which resources are effective or more effective. Moreover, resources are not simply effective or ineffective. They are effective or ineffective with respect to our objectives. I have no cure for the complexity of the world other than to recommend that simple metrics be avoided and complex issues be thoroughly discussed so that they are understood as well as we finite humans can understand them.

Many questions of resource allocation pose questions of fairness (see Strike, 1988). These questions can be of quite different sorts. The band needs new music and the football team new uniforms, but we cannot provide both. What is fair? A central issue of fairness concerns the resource commitment we should make to students with high needs. Disabled students such as Carli are one example. Students who come from highly disadvantaged backgrounds are another. These students often require significantly more resources to produce adequate educational gains. Should we invest more in these students? Should we do so even when our investments pay modest dividends and we might benefit more from other uses of our scarce resources? Should we put our resources where they will have the largest impact? And what does this mean?

Two examples: First, imagine that you have to choose between the expansion of a program for gifted and talented students and a program to provide special tutoring for those students who are two grades behind in reading. Second, imagine that you are asked to choose between adding a new teacher to work with students who, like Carli, are afflicted with autism and adding a new teacher to improve your school's music program.

Now consider three different approaches to how to think about these matters.

Resource Allocation and Benefit Maximization

Suppose we think like a utilitarian. We will apply the principle of benefit maximization. What we want is the greatest good for the greatest number, the most bang for the buck.

How will we decide what counts as the *bang* of more bang for the buck? It is often difficult to know which expenditure of resources produces the most good. Even if we limit our concerns to economic outcomes, it is hard to know what the long-term consequences of our decisions will be. In our first example, it may be that if we invest in a gifted and talented program, we will produce successful scientists and entrepreneurs who will add to the vitality of the American economy and make everyone better off in the process. But it may also be that these students would succeed quite well without extra resources. Perhaps providing a special program for these students produces little real long-term gain and largely contributes only to the current satisfaction of these students. Should we invest more in them, even if only to reduce their boredom?

If we invest in the remedial reading program and even if we only manage to produce one year's gain in reading ability in our target population, this may be enough to enable many of these students to complete high school and become gainfully employed. They may not become scientists or business people, but they might become good citizens and good parents. How are we to know? Perhaps we can measure immediate results and decide if either program adds to the achievement of the students it serves, but how are we to gauge these long-term outcomes? That is what the principle of benefit maximization requires us to do.

The choice between a music teacher and a special education teacher suggests a second problem. Here we are investing in very different kinds of outcomes. Music may enrich the lives of many students. It may also help them develop friendships and gain a sense of accomplishment when they are able to perform well. In the case of special education, we may be investing in increased functionality that may allow people to become more self-sufficient, but we may also be investing in the capacity to form more adequate relationships or in human dignity. How are we to compare such different goods as music appreciation, self-sufficiency, adequate relationships, and dignity?

Here, then, we see two difficulties of trying to use the principle of benefit maximization as a principle of resource allocation in education. Often it is unclear how we are to compare benefits of very different types. If we can achieve some clarity about this, the range of consequences of our actions spread, like ripples on a pond, beyond our ability to fully grasp them. It is very difficult to decide what produces the greatest good for the greatest number.And there is another, more severe problem. The principle of benefit maximization takes into account the amount of benefit produced but does not take into account how this benefit is distributed. We can see why this is important by revising our examples.

Suppose we now compare expending resources on a program for the gifted and talented versus expending them on a program for severely disabled children. And suppose also that we know at least that we will get more economic bang for our buck if we spend our resources on the gifted and talented.

Does this decide the matter? It does not. It seems unreasonable to view the provision of resources for disabled students (especially severely disabled students) primarily as an economic investment. As a rule, when we view educational resources as economic investments, we wish to invest resources in their most efficient use, and this is what the principle of benefit maximization requires. In many cases, this will lead us to view investment in disabled students as a poor investment simply because we can get more bang for our buck elsewhere.

Of course, this depends on what we count as a bang. We need not focus on economic outcome. Nevertheless, the problem persists. No matter what we count as a bang, the principle of benefit maximization seeks to maximize the average and is insensitive to the distribution of benefits. And it will shortchange those who benefit less from an investment in favor of those who benefit more. It will reward ability to profit over need.

Consider that it is common for people to argue that we should invest in special education because the cost of educating disabled students is less than the cost of their lifetime care. We save a great deal over the long haul by helping disabled children to become self-sufficient. However, this argument is weak. Not all disabled children can achieve self-sufficiency. For those who cannot, shall we not invest in their education at all? The principle of benefit maximization seems to suggest this. Moreover, the principle of benefit maximization does not require us to invest in programs that produce a benefit. It requires us to make the most efficient investment. The question is not, then, whether an investment in disabled children produces some benefit or even a significant benefit. It is whether it produces the most benefit when compared to other investments.

What if there are more efficient investments than investing in the education of disabled children? Should we deny an education to these children when there are better (more efficient) uses for our resources? Again, the principle of benefit maximization requires that we maximize the benefits produced, but it is indifferent to how they are distributed. Hence, it has the potential to reduce benefits to high-needs students if there are other uses of resources that produce larger outcomes.

This result shows the weakness of the principle of benefit maximization, especially if we focus on economic benefits. We must view disabled people as people with needs, with families who love them, and as human beings entitled to an education that allows them to develop their capacities, regardless of whether these capacities will be brought to the service of the economy. Sometimes the investment in special education is an investment in dignity and humane treatment, not in economic development.

To Each According to Their Need

Perhaps, then, we should consider a different standard. Suppose we say that instead of investing resources in those programs most likely to produce the greatest overall benefit, we invest so as to prefer those students with the greatest need. This, too, has its problems.

Just as it is unclear what is to count as a *benefit* or how we compare quite different benefits, it is not always clear what we count as *need* and how we compare different kinds of needs. Intuitively, it seems obvious that students with disabilities or students raised in high poverty environments have greater needs than other students, but who has the greater need when we compare these two groups of students? Could we decide whether to invest in programs for students raised in poverty or in programs for students with disabilities by deciding who has the greater need? This is not quite so clear.

And other students may claim to have needs. It is often argued that gifted and talented students have a need for intellectual stimulation that is not satisfied by typical academic programs. How great is this need? How shall we compare it to the needs of disadvantaged or disabled students?

We should also consider that, while we may not be wholly devoted to maximizing good outcomes, we cannot be altogether oblivious to them, either. In some cases, disadvantaged or disabled students can require a considerable expenditure of resources for very modest gains. At what point do such expenditures of resources impose an unreasonable burden on those who must provide them or on those other students who will receive less because others receive more? I do not know the answer to these questions, but we cannot direct resources to those with the greater need without considering the benefits likely to result and without considering the needs of others.

It seems that "to each according to their need" is no more adequate as a principle of resource allocation than "to each according to the benefit they produce."

Funding Just and Reasonable Aspirations

Consider a third standard. Suppose that, when we consider what different students need and what they are entitled to, we begin by asking ourselves what capacities it is desirable for them to acquire given their current life situation, their potential level of functioning (particularly in the case of disabled students), and their reasonable and just aspirations. We then seek to provide resources for these reasonable and just aspirations.

For the majority of students, we might come up with a package of desired capacities varying only slightly with ability and aspirations. We will want most students to succeed on those things that public schools teach. We may, however, vary the resources committed to different groups of students depending on what is required to realize these capacities.

For special needs students, we may come up with a different set of educational aspirations, depending on what different students are capable of achieving. This is part of what we are asked to do when we develop an IEP for special students. Once we determine what capacities are to be desired and can be hoped for, we can consider a package of resources that provides each student a fair chance to achieve these desired capacities. (This view is suggested by Kittay [1999], although it is not quite her view.)

We do not commit ourselves to fully realizing everyone's potential. That is impossible, and it places no constraints on the demands that might be made for resources. We aim at what is possible given the resources we have. We do not deny resources to anyone on the basis of projections about their future productivity. Nor do we resist providing more resources to some students than others because the costs of achieving the package of capacities we aspire to for them may cost more than the package we aspire to for other students. We aim at a fair share of resources rooted in an assessment of what is possible and desirable.

This third view (toward which I incline) has some of the deficiencies of the others. It is certainly not precise. Its application will require judgment. At the same time, it is shaped by some considerations that we have developed in the course of the argument. It recognizes the importance of getting some benefit from the resources we expend, but it does not deny resources when there are more efficient alternative uses. It recognizes need, but it does not permit need to absorb resources when there is little benefit. It also defines need in terms of the acquisition of desired and possible capacities, not merely in terms of the intensity of wants.

What it requires is that educators make judgments about what is desirable and possible for students whose needs may be quite different and provide a fair and appropriate portion of educational resources intended to help students achieve these capacities. Perhaps one way of saying this is to suggest that in the minds of educators, if not on paper or in law, every student should have an IEP.

We can justify such a view by an appeal to the principles of equal respect and community. When we look at resource allocation from the principle of equal respect, we are reminded that the duty to respect all people is not dependent on their particular capacities and potential. Those who are disabled or have high educational needs are persons entitled to equal respect. Were we or one of our loved ones similarly in need, we would want resources adequate to develop capacities.

When we look at high-needs students from the perspective of the principle of community, we reach a similar conclusion. Our communities are better and stronger when all are cared for. Caring for the weakest among us expresses our commitment to live in good communities where individuals are valued as members and not solely because of what they can contribute to our own welfare. We cannot simply deduce what resources should be available to high-needs students from these principles. But they may serve to guide our response to the special circumstances of each case.

What might the implications be for Carli? To make a firm judgment about her case, one would need to know more detail about her situation than I have provided. However, we can say some things. It seems likely that it is reasonable to aspire to a higher level of functioning for Carli than her current IEP and the resources committed to her education currently envision. Carli has shown that she responds well to an educational program and that she is not responding well to her current program.

Moreover, the cost of what her parents wish for her is not unreasonable. They want more of the time of a special teacher already assigned to work with Carli. They are not asking that her tuition be paid to an expensive private school or that she have a special teacher dedicated to meeting only her needs. This makes a strong case that she is entitled to the resources required to expand her educational program. It is not a conclusive case because we do not know where these resources will come from and what other needs will go unmet. But we do know that the affirmative case for Carli is strong.

EQUALITY, COMMUNITY, AND DIVERSITY: THE IDEA OF COMMUNITY

In your school, you have been concerned about the competitive spirit that some of your students bring to their studies, and you have tried to create a sense of community by using cooperative learning strategies. This has been a mixed success and has generated some resistance and racial discord. What is a community? Why care about community?

Think of an orchestra. One of the characteristics of orchestras is that they succeed or fail as a group. It is the orchestra that plays well. While there are individual members of the orchestra, they must also play together. To do so they must adopt a shared interpretation of the music, respect a collective view of how the music is to be played, and follow the conductor. Individual interests must be subservient to common ends and shared goals. Cooperation is required. This is true not only of orchestras, but of other groups that have what I shall call a *shared project*. A shared project involves shared ends which require cooperation to achieve.

Members of orchestras benefit from one another's excellence. If I play the oboe and I wish my orchestra to play well, I must value violinists and tuba players. It is in my interest to help them play well. My relationship with other members of the orchestra is not competitive. In competitive relationships I benefit not only from my successes, but from the failures of my competitors. In orchestras, I succeed when others succeed. The fundamental fact about orchestras is, "We are all in this together."

This does not banish competition. Members of orchestras may compete for chairs, solos, or recognition. They may be motivated by personal goals. Nevertheless, if the orchestra is to play well, individual goals must be subservient to group goals. Competition, while real, is not at the heart of the matter.

An orchestra is an exemplar of a community. Communities have members. These members are necessarily diverse—we would not have an orchestra if we had only oboe players—but they must also seek a certain form of unity. Members of communities have certain relationships with one another and with the community. Loyalty and solidarity are the principal commitments that characterize these relationships. Loyalty and solidarity are at the center of the sense that we are all in this together. Loyalty and solidarity often begin in a commitment to the ends of the community, but in good communities, they grow to include ties of caring and commitment to members of the community that go beyond achieving the ends of the community.

We see this all the time in schools. Students who are members of musical groups and sports teams form bonds of friendship with one another. They come to care about one another in ways that go well beyond the need to work together to achieve the ends of the community. At some point, they may learn to find some of their own happiness in the well-being of others. That, too, is a benefit.

Another value that can be associated with community is trust. When the relationships among people are competitive, we can only trust people if we believe that their personal integrity is strong enough to overcome their desire to achieve their own private ends. If Jones can benefit by lying to Smith, Smith can only trust Jones if he believes that Jones cares more for truthfulness than for the benefits to be gained by lying. If, however, Smith and Jones are members of a community, there are additional reasons for trust. One is that Smith and Jones want the same thing, and they can only attain what they want by cooperation. A second reason is that Smith and Jones may be bonded together by relationships of loyalty, solidarity, and friendship. They value one another and care for their relationship. Hence, they will not wish to lie and see no benefit to themselves in doing so.

Good communities have these four characteristics:

1. They have shared ends that can only be achieved through the cooperation of members.

2. Communities tend to succeed or fail collectivity rather than as individuals.

3. In communities, members benefit from the growth of the capacity of other members and the commitment of other members to the community's goals.

4. In communities, members are bound together by ties of loyalty, solidarity, and trust.

Can we think of classrooms or schools as though they were communities? I think we can. We want our students to be good citizens, to be able to live an examined life, and to master some craft or skill that enhances the quality of their experience. Our classrooms should be sites of collective inquiry, and our schools learning communities. These various goals are all like the goals of orchestras. We often succeed or fail as a group, and the success of each contributes to the success of all. Three examples:

1. First, if one goal of a school is to promote the capacity to lead an examined life, then the ability of members of the school community to articulate views of good living and to participate in their discussion and evaluation must be valued. Leading an examined life is, as Socrates demonstrated long ago, an activity that requires discussion, argument, and debate. If we are serious about the examined life, we should value the capacity of those individuals who are able to stimulate, challenge, and assist us in the process of reflection on the question of how we should live. Pursuing the examined life is a process where we can find community in diversity of opinion and where each benefits from the capacity of others. This is a process in which all members of the classroom or the school benefit when others receive a good education.

2. Second, students should be able to acquire what I have called the cognitive prerequisites to appreciate experience. These prerequisites are to be found, in part, in the school's official curriculum. Art and music, math and science, sport and craft; all can be learned so as to enhance the capacity to enjoy experience. But the resources for the enhancement of experience are also to be found in our various cultures. Each culture possesses ways of seeing and appreciating the world that provide learning opportunities that can enrich the experience of others. Sharing these resources is another way in which each can contribute to the enrichment of all.

3. Third, consider citizenship. A good society is one in which people recognize that they share a common fate and work together to achieve common goods. Good neighborhoods, towns, and cities require functional government, good public transportation, parks, shared recreational opportunities, civic organizations, community associations, clubs, choirs, congregations, and volunteer fire companies.

These are among the things that contribute to the common good. They require a spirit of cooperation and a recognition that each benefits from the participation and competence of all. They are quickly destroyed if we are unwilling to engage in activities that benefit others as well as ourselves. Good government is undermined if we view it as "war by other means," that is, if we view government primarily as the forum in which struggles among different individuals for resources and privileges is waged. Good citizens are people who serve their communities. The essence of a good citizen is a commitment to the common good.

COMMUNITY AND EQUALITY

What does this have to do with equality? To answer this question, consider first that members of liberal democratic societies stand in many and diverse relations to one another. Two broad kinds of relationships are implicit in what I have said above. First, liberal democratic societies are committed to the view that people have a right to their own conception of their own lives. Free people may freely choose their own religions, occupations, and lifestyles.

Our ability to realize our conception of the good requires scarce resources. If we are to succeed, we need wealth and income and, therefore, the opportunity to obtain the jobs and the qualifications on which wealth and income depend. We need to find a place in the economy. Economic activity is a form of social cooperation. Even in economic activity we all benefit when other people are able to be productive. Nevertheless, obtaining a place in the economy is in large measure a competitive matter.

In education, competition is at the heart of the activity of obtaining qualifications and finding a satisfactory place in the economy. Hence, liberal democratic societies recognize that free people are legitimately different; they respect each other's choices, and they attempt to create fair conditions of cooperation that include the ability to compete for scarce resources and opportunities on a fair and equal basis. Fair competition is what equal opportunity is about.

At the same time, we must also see ourselves as citizens of a democratic society where we pursue certain common goods and the common good. Our democracy is stronger and our communities better if we see ourselves as "all in it together," recognize the benefits of social cooperation toward the common good, and value the capacity and the commitment of each to the common good.

Hence, in liberal democratic societies, we stand in two relationships to one another. We are competitors for the resources and opportunities on which our individual projects depend, and we are fellow citizens cooperating in pursuit of common goods and the creation of a strong democratic society. How does this affect our understanding of equality in education?

I can best develop this by discussing cooperative learning. Cooperative learning involves learning through teamwork. Students learn together by pursuing a learning project together. Often, cooperative learning involves getting a common grade for a commonly produced product. Hence, students succeed or fail together.

Note two initial facts. First, one of the difficulties in employing cooperative learning strategies is that some students do not wish to engage in them. They may feel that other students in the group are a drag on their mastery of material. I have employed cooperative learning projects in one university course I taught for many years. I justified this to students by claiming that when they became teachers they would need to know how to work together as members of a learning community. Most students accepted this, but there were also regularly some who wished to do an individual project, arguing that they could learn more on their own, and there were always a few who exploited the effort of others.

This suggests a second point. One difficulty with cooperative learning is that in many cases in school situations, the fact that students succeed as a group is artificially created and may seem unfair. In my class, the cooperative projects students pursued required a single product (a report), and students received a common grade. Here the fact that they succeeded or failed as a group was created by me. I could have assigned each student a paper to do. I might have permitted them to share the work but to submit an individual report. In this way, cooperative learning projects are not like orchestras or sports teams, where the fact that they succeed or fail as a group is in some sense naturally occurring.

That cooperative learning projects will seem to some students as artificially contrived is at the heart of these problems. Some students may feel that they are carrying others. Some may seek to exploit the work of others because they can gain the benefit of the work of others at no cost to themselves. This does not show that cooperative learning is not valuable. What it shows is that cooperative learning requires that students enter into cooperative projects with the perspective that emphasizes that we are all in this together. To have such a perspective is to feel a sense of commitment to the other members of the group, to think it to be a good thing if others gain from one's effort and vice versa.

Cooperative learning may help to create such an outlook. Both cooperation and competition involve attitudes toward others that are learned. It should not be surprising that some students resist cooperative learning if the message schools routinely communicate about learning is that it is an individual affair in which one pursues one's own welfare in competition with others. On the other hand, if cooperation is emphasized from the outset and if the mutual benefits and common goods of learning are emphasized, students are more likely to enter into cooperative learning situations with a sense that we are all in this together.

What follows is that cooperative learning is most likely to be successful if educators give appropriate weight to those educational goals where it is most likely that there is significant mutual benefit from the success of all. Most educational goals, even the economic goals, have some element of this, but a sense of common citizenship in a common democratic community seems to me to be central.

What does this have to do with equality? At least three things: First, if classrooms have a strong sense of community permeated with the conviction that we are all in this together, then we are more likely to succeed in creating equality of opportunity. Students will find it appropriate that they function as educational resources for one another and will see the benefit to themselves when it is literally true that no child is left behind.

Second, suppose that we approach questions of resource allocation in the way suggested by the third approach I sketched above, that is, we determine for each child an appropriate level of capacities to be acquired and the level of resources required for a fair chance to achieve these capacities. And suppose that for some children, special needs require a disproportionately large set of resources. If we have managed to communicate a sense that we are all in it together, we may hope that people will view these resources not as a drain on the resources invested in their own education but as an investment of resources in someone whose growth and success benefits us all. Investment of resources in high-needs students can be viewed as an investment in community.

The third benefit of a strong sense of community so far as equality is concerned is that it provides a useful perspective on multiculturalism.

COMMUNITY AND DIVERSITY

American educators seem generally to believe in a multicultural society, yet it is often quite difficult to say what this means. It is tempting to say that one thing we mean is that we want to treat all cultures equally, but we do not really mean that. After all, it makes quite good sense to say that the Mafia has a culture, that Enron was characterized by a culture of greed, or that there is such a thing as a drug culture. Presumably, we do not wish to claim that we should treat such cultures with the same degree of respect with which we would treat the cultures of the various ethnic groups in the United States.

Moreover, the United States has a political culture that is shaped, in part, by its traditions and by the Constitution. We ask people who wish to become U.S. citizens to express their loyalty to the Constitution and the U.S. form of government. When people immigrate to the United States, we do not expect them to abandon all of the culture of their nation of origin, but we do expect them to adopt something of our political culture, to use U.S. currency in most of their economic activity, to learn English, and to obey our laws. While these things are a part of our culture, no one really expects multiculturalism to apply to them.

But the people who comprise the citizens of the United States do come from a remarkably large number of places. They are of different races, religions, and ethnic groups. They may have different tastes in food, dress, or music. How are we to view these differences?

First, we should note that identity is often shaped by and linked to culture. People may think of themselves as Latino, African American, or Mung, and these identifications are not merely facts about them. They are part of who they are. One implication of this is that it is difficult to show respect for people while at the same time not respecting or disrespecting their culture. We cannot easily claim to respect individuals as persons while believing that their religion is nothing but superstition, that their people have contributed nothing of value to human society, that their music is noise, that their celebrations are meaningless, and that their food is inedible or tasteless. If we are to show respect for the students in our schools, we must recognize and show respect for those aspects of culture that are identity shaping (see Taylor, 1994).

Recognition requires inclusion. We must include the culture of those who are members of the school community in the curriculum of the school. History must be taught so as to include the contribution of all groups present. Literature must include the literature of those present.

Showing respect means that we must seek to attach value to what is included. This is a notion that requires care. Sometimes showing respect means to honor the worth of a contribution. Sometimes it may require that we identify with the suffering of others. When we are concerned with matters such as religion, respect does not require us to agree that the religion of others is just as true as our own; instead, it requires that we view the beliefs of others as convictions they hold with integrity and as making a claim for our consideration. We may not believe the religions of others, but we should not view them as acceptable only by those who are ignorant or evil.

Respect, it should be added, does not require us to lie or to teach feel-good history. It does not preclude us from appraising the art, music, or literature of other groups. What it requires is an attitude of openness and a willingness to understand what others see, think, and feel, and to be open to appreciation of the work of others.

A second aspect of multiculturalism is that we must avoid the idea that some of us own the curriculum and others are guests. Equality in multicultural societies cannot mean open access to a curriculum that has been created for and expresses the view of a dominant group. If a curriculum is to show recognition and respect for all, it must be one that cannot be represented as the expression of the culture of one group with occasional concessions that recognize the presence of others. The best way to achieve such a curriculum is to have fair and equal participation of all in its construction. Hence, democracy is at the core of multiculturalism.

A third point concerning multiculturalism is that every culture has two important needs. The first is the need to reproduce. The second is the need to interact. The need to reproduce is obvious. Cultures whose members fail to transmit their culture to the next generation cease to exist. Cultures become extinct if they cannot reproduce. This means that every culture requires effective means to communicate with its younger generation. While this seems obvious, we should consider that it is a requirement that large multicultural societies can make difficult for minority cultures. Even when the major institutions of the society provide minority cultures with recognition and respect, that may not be sufficient to transmit the culture. Minority cultures may require institutions they control.

Public schools are often not adequate to secure the conditions required for transmission of minority cultures. Nor, in general, should they be expected to create these conditions. Yet they should not make the process of cultural transmission more difficult, and they may assist in the process of cultural transmission when that is feasible. Teaching courses in African American history in schools where there are many African Americans is an obvious example.

Interaction is also required. Cultures grow and learn through interaction. Some of the vices to which cultures may be susceptible, such as parochialism, ossification, and intolerance, are cured through interaction. In America, the results of cultural interaction and exchange are everywhere. We speak in languages that have roots in many tongues that have gone before. We count using a number system developed by Arabs. Music with African roots is played on instruments with origins in Europe and elsewhere. Most of the religions to which Americans subscribe have their origins in the Middle East, although our understanding of them has been filtered through Greek philosophy.

Useful technologies tend to spread rapidly among cultures. It is thus a significant error to view cultures as isolated and static or as sharply distinct from one another. It is similarly an error to wish this to be so. While some measure of isolation may be necessary to preserve some cultures, as a rule, isolation has undesirable consequences. It retards the growth of the isolated group. It prevents others from learning from the isolated culture, and it restricts the life options of the members of the isolated group.

The principal lesson of these brief comments should be that in creating multicultural classrooms and schools, we should emphasize cross-cultural sharing and dialogue. The aim should be to learn from one another. Indeed, there is little that expresses recognition and respect for a culture as well as the desire to learn what it has to teach.

Earlier in this chapter, I argued two points that need to be recalled. First, I argued that while equal opportunity was essentially a view of what counted as fair competition, nevertheless, schools were more likely to succeed in promoting equal opportunity if they encouraged the view that we are all in this together. Second, I suggested that the pursuit of two goals of education was especially able to encourage such an outlook. The first of these goals is citizenship, where students should learn to see themselves as cooperating together in a common democratic project in pursuit of the common good. The second is an examined life, where the ideas, criticism, and cultures of others are viewed as assets and resources for self-reflection and self-enrichment.

Note how these ideas hang together with multicultural education. When we think of multicultural education as requiring recognition and respect, we are led to think of the school's curriculum as a cooperative democratic project in which we retain our differences when we wish, learn from one another when we can, and work together to achieve common goods and create a shared democratic culture in which all are respected and none dominated or oppressed. This is one way in which we are all in it together. In this shared multicultural project, we are also in it together in that through our interaction, each contributes to the welfare of all by being a resource for the examined life and for the expansion of cultural opportunities.

School leaders need to approach their tasks with two visions of equality. One is equality of opportunity. Students are viewed as in competition for further opportunities, positions, and income. The goal is to make the competition fair. The second is equality within a multicultural community. Here the goal is to engage students in a shared project to construct a democratic community and lead the examined life.

In a way, in suggesting these ideas I am returning us to *Brown v. Board of Education*. *Brown* is not exactly about self-esteem. Rather, *Brown* is about a conception of equality that aspires to the equal recognition of all as citizens. However, in outlawing state-imposed segregation, *Brown* takes only the first step toward including all in a democratic society that gives recognition and respect to all and avoids domination and oppression. To complete that project, we need an educational system that views each as having something of worth to contribute to the benefit of all.

CONCLUSIONS

The school leader who wishes to promote an equal education in an age of accountability should approach the task with three big ideas.

The first idea is that educational outcomes and the life prospects that are contingent on them should not depend on morally arbitrary characteristics such as race, ethnicity, socioeconomic class, or gender. This commitment, properly understood, will lead to a commitment that schools, insofar as they are able, should eliminate the effects of these characteristics on achievement.

The second idea is that, while test scores that measure achievement in selected areas are a useful measure of the extent to which equal opportunity has been achieved, they do not exhaust its meaning. Educators and school leaders must be committed to realizing a larger conception of education in the lives of their students—one in which citizenship, the examined life, and the acquisition of capacities that enable students to appreciate experience all have weight. It is this conception of education that must be equalized. We may not reduce the education made available to minority or disadvantaged students so as to focus more exclusively on raising test scores.

Third, community is important. If we can create a sense that we are all in it together, many of the goals of education become easier to achieve, including equal opportunity and multiculturalism. Moreover, when the relationships among students and their families are shaped by values such as loyalty and belonging, it is easier to achieve an environment in which students learn from one another and adequate resources are available to meet the needs of our most vulnerable members.

Constitutional Essentials, Part III

Democracy, Community, and Accountability

That this nation under God shall have a new birth of freedom and that government of the people, for the people, and by the people, shall not perish from the earth.

—Abraham Lincoln, the Gettysburg Address (Bartlett, 1955)

This is the essence of the New Compact for Learning: that schools and school districts exercise initiative to make what changes may be needed to bring about the learning results we all desire. In a new relationship between the State and localities, the State defines more precisely what is to be learned, and local teachers, administrators, and boards of education have more freedom to decide how such learning is to occur.

—*A New Compact for Learning* (1994, p. 10)

PROLOGUE AND SCENARIO

Democracy is not just an effective way of making decisions; it is a way of legitimating them. Members of democratic societies would be unlikely to accept the decisions of a monarch even if those decisions were routinely wise and produced good outcomes. We would believe that these decisions were illegitimate because they were not properly made. They were made without our consent and participation. Such decisions are undemocratic even if they are wise.

Democracy is not a single thing. Educational leaders are often expected to be democratic leaders and to create democratic communities in their schools. They are also expected to obey the decisions of democratically elected legislatures, school boards, and state legislatures. As we shall see, these expectations may be in tension because they tap into different conceptions of democracy.

There are other legitimization norms in addition to those of democracy. A democratic decision may not be legitimate if it violates someone's rights. Rights may restrict the range of democratic decisions. Sometimes decisions should be made by those who are most knowledgeable. As Plato (1962) once argued, "Those who know should rule."

As a school leader, your response to various actors and voices in your school and your view of your role as a leader depend on how you understand the notion of legitimate authority and legitimate decision making and how this understanding positions you in relationship to others. Legitimization norms also shape how you understand the kind of community you wish your school to be.

In this chapter, I will return to our initial scenario and expand it so that we can consider some views of how decisions are legitimated. I will also use these discussions to develop an expanded conception of accountability. When we hold people accountable, we hold them accountable for something and to someone. The currently conventional view of accountability assumes that educators are to be held accountable for raising test scores to legislatures—the elected representatives of the people. Both views are too narrow.

In Chapter 1, I asked you to imagine that you are the leader of a successful school in a less-than-successful, large district. The board of education has required that every school in your district closely align its curriculum with state standards and has insisted that a certain amount of instructional time be spent on test review. The parents and teachers in your school are unhappy about this. They fear that it may undermine what they see as a good instructional program.

I want you now to consider two letters that have been written to you about this: one from your teachers and one from a group of parents. These letters ask you to behave as a democratic leader who is open to their input. Other norms of legitimate authority are also assumed in these letters. Our task in this chapter is to tease out these norms and to examine them. Understanding these norms is the key to a reasonable view of community and accountability.

Here is the letter from the teachers:

We have considered the board's new policy on testing. It is our professional judgment that these mandates are not consistent with good education and will harm our students. Our current instructional strategy is supported by research and our own experience. We have met regularly to discuss the implementation of our curriculum and the instructional strategies it requires. We have experimented with it and modified it. We have consulted with parents and community members. We have achieved a consensus, one that parents have bought into, that this is the best program for our students. We have become what you have urged us to become—a collegial and democratic learning community. We want the best for our children, and we work hard and collectively to assure ourselves that all our children are learning. We leave no child behind. Our children do well on state tests, and they achieve these results without our teaching to the test and without distortion of our curriculum. Our professional duty is to put the welfare of our students first.

Now you are asking us to revise our excellent program so that we can engage in endless drills and test preparation. We are to do this to accommodate our program to the ill-considered demands of a group of ignorant and self-serving politicians who have no regard for our children and who have chosen an educational strategy more notable for its sound bites than for its wisdom.

Our professional integrity will not permit us to comply. We demand that you present our case for exemption from these policies to the school board and, if they are unwilling to agree, that you help us to subvert their demands. If you are the democratic leader you claim to be, you will honor our request.

The supporting letter from the parents follows:

We agree with our teachers that the new board policies are unwise. We are not opposed to accountability or testing. We are concerned, however, with the proposed changes in instruction. Our teachers have worked with us in planning this program. We all believe in it. We work with our children to further its goals. We help them with their homework, and we volunteer at the school. We are an integral part of the school community and its work. Now we must defend what we have collectively achieved.

These children are our children. That we send them to you does not mean that you have our permission to do whatever you want with them. You educate them with our approval and as our agent. You do not have our permission to adopt educational practices that are harmful to them.

This is a free country. Its people are citizens, not subjects. First and foremost you are accountable to us. We have discussed this matter thoroughly and have democratically achieved a collective opinion that the board's policies are unacceptable. We insist that you resist the school board's ill-considered mandates. We will assist you in any way we can. If you are not able to do this, we will have to consider keeping our children home on testing days.

These letters are complex, as well as intemperate. They make substantive arguments concerning the merits of your current program and the perceived demerits of the board's views. But they also invoke various norms of legitimate authority. The teachers claim to be a professional community. The parents claim that their view of how to educate their children should be given top priority. Both groups appeal to norms of democracy to justify their claims. The teachers suggest that if you are a democratic leader, you will do what they wish.

Democracy, professionalism, collegiality, parents' rights—it seems that if you do not do what the parents and teachers want, you will offend against all that is right and just. And then there is the school board that was duly elected and that pays your salary. How will you sort through these conflicting norms? To whom are you accountable?

DEMOCRATIC COMMUNITY AND DEMOCRATIC LEADERSHIP

It is generally supposed to be a good thing if school leaders are democratic leaders. What does that mean? It might mean that school leaders are elected, but clearly that is incorrect. In the United States, school leaders in public schools are appointed officials.

Perhaps democratic leaders should submit their decisions to a vote. Perhaps this does occur. Leaders may conduct meetings in which faculty vote on appropriate matters. Perhaps some matters are submitted to parents. But such procedures are not common. Nor is it obvious that they are either required or desirable.

Perhaps we mean something like this when we speak of democratic leaders: A democratic leader is one who considers the views of others, who listens to parents and teachers, who treats people with respect, who is open to suggestions, and who delegates or distributes responsibility. Such leaders are not autocratic or authoritarian. They are democratic. But what makes this democratic? After all, a good king might do as much. This notion of democratic leadership gives others voice but not authority.

Sometimes we think of democratic leaders as people who create democratic organizations, and we juxtapose democratic organizations either to authoritarian or bureaucratic ones. An organization is bureaucratic when it is hierarchical and rule-governed and when authority is a function of assigned roles within the bureaucracy. It is democratic when it is "flat," egalitarian, and when decisions tend to be made consensually.

If this is what we mean, then we should note that school leaders get their formal authority from the roles they occupy, not from their teachers or their parents. Like it or not, school leaders are part of a hierarchy of authority that draws its legitimacy from the fact that it serves an elected legislature. This is not a fact about leadership style. It is a matter of law.

Should we view public schools as undemocratic because they are hierarchical and bureaucratic? This is commonly claimed, but it does not follow. Much of the confusing way we tend to talk about leaders as democratic or undemocratic flows from a failure to be clear about what democracy is.

Consider a provisional definition of a democracy. Suppose that we view a democracy as a certain type of community, a "polity," that makes decisions in a way that respects the political equality of all citizens. For now let us suppose that political equality consists of at least two things: First, people have equal interests. No one is inherently entitled to better treatment than anyone else. Second, people are entitled to a fair say in decision-making. Given this, how are democratic decisions made? Consider two criteria:

1. Decisions are made democratically when the interests of all citizens of the polity are fairly considered.

2. Decisions are made democratically when all citizens of the polity have a fair chance to influence decisions via voice and/or authority.

In undemocratic states, the interests of some count more than the interests of others. This is why states in which slavery is practiced are undemocratic. But states can be undemocratic in other, less dramatic, ways. A theocracy would be undemocratic insofar as the interests of unbelievers counted for less than the interests of believers. A society may be undemocratic if the rich receive favored treatment over the poor. In a democratic society, those who rule must do so in the interest of all. Democracy seeks the common good and the good of all equally.

Yet the fair consideration of interests is not sufficient to characterize a democracy. A benevolent monarchy might respect the interests of all, but that would not make a monarchy into a democracy. Democracy also requires that citizens have voice with respect to decisions. Moreover, voice is not enough. What seems required in addition is some right to participate in decision making. Kings may be good listeners. Democracy requires that everyone's views carry authority.

Is this adequate to define democracy? Lincoln characterized democracy as a government of the people, by the people, and for the people. Others have characterized democracy as a government that rests on the consent of the governed. A government that considers the interests of all equally might be said to be a government for the people. One where people participate in public debates about law and policy and in which their views and their votes carry authority might be said to be of the people and to rest on the consent of the governed. A government in which citizens have a right to run for and to hold office might be viewed as a government by the people. A democratic society, thus, has these essential features: It rules in the interests of everyone. It has institutions where people can make their views heard. It has institutions that grant to individuals proportional authority over decision making. And it permits all citizens to stand for office.

Americans often consider a government to be democratic when those who rule are elected. Is this adequate? Elections conducted under the norm of one person, one vote, can be viewed as giving citizens proportional authority. The debates that generally precede elections provide opportunity for voice. The fact that, to be elected, politicians need to attend to the interests of at least a majority of citizens, together with the fact that there are many types of interests that often do not align themselves with one group to the exclusion of others, means that representative democracies at least tend to consider the interests of all. That voting occurs can be viewed as meaning that those who win have the consent of the governed (including those who vote for losing candidates, whose consent is expressed through participation or at least the opportunity to participate). And all citizens can run for office.

Of course, representative democracies meet the requirements of democracy imperfectly. In large political communities, influence and voice are proportionately reduced. Reasoned argument about the public interest may be replaced by political advertising and sound bites, and small but cohesive groups may employ the electoral system to impose their will on minorities or even majorities and fail to give adequate expression to the interests of all. When voice depends on money, the rich may dominate or wield disproportionate influence. In capitalist societies, there is always the risk that the government will become a plutocracy. All of these are vices of representative democracy.

How might these weaknesses be diminished? The size of the political community might be reduced. If democratic communities consisted (say) of a few hundred people rather than thousands or millions, opportunities for voice, participation, and influence would be considerably enhanced. People could be heard directly, perhaps in town meetings. Arguments could be worked through with ample time for discussion and debate. Disagreements might be among friends and neighbors, and the will to compromise thereby enhanced. There would be more opportunity to successfully stand for office.

We might also place greater emphasis on consensus, reason, and the common good as essential features of democratic deliberation. Representative democracies tend to "vector" interests. They seek to balance competing interests more than they seek to reconcile or resolve them. But we might hope for democratic processes in which people value not only their own good, but that of others, and where rational discourse seeks for the common good.

These democratic processes and practices would seek for consensus and "the power of the better argument" rather than for a packaging of conflicting interests in which everyone gets a piece and no one is shut out.

This kind of deliberation might be thought to be more likely in smaller democratic communities. (This conception owes much to the work of Jurgen Habermas [1984] and his notion of an ideal speech community.)

This view also has certain problems. If most decisions were made by the discussions of small groups, it would be difficult to know how decisions that affect large groups would be legitimately made. Moreover, small groups would be able to make decisions that affected the members of large groups without their consent. Defense is an example of the first problem. It is hard to see how national defense could be cared for by the democratic processes of small groups.

Schools are often examples of the second problem. If America were a nation of small towns and if people tended to live where they were born, it might make sense for all educational decisions to be made locally by those whom they immediately affect. But we are not such a nation. We are a mobile people. Students frequently attend multiple schools in multiple communities. Even when they do not, they are not likely to work or to live in the same community where they attended school. And even if they do, their economic skills and capacity to be good citizens affect people well beyond their local community.

In short, even in education, which has traditionally been governed locally, local decisions have consequences for many beyond the local community. If educational decision making occurred entirely at the local level, then local citizens would have the power to impose consequences on people who live elsewhere without their participation or consent.

Do we have two different views of democracy—one that emphasizes elections and representation and a second that emphasizes deliberation, consensus, and local participation? This overstates the matter. Let us say, rather, that we have two strains in democratic thought, one that emphasizes representation and elections (representative democracy) and one that emphasizes local deliberation and participation (democratic localism). The trick, I believe, is how to combine their best features.

Note four things here. First, in the United States, the fundamental institutions of democracy are those of representative democracy. In education, citizens elect people to represent them. These representatives (or their agents) hire school leaders to carry out their policies and educate our children.

Second, the central commitment of representative democracy is to the sovereignty of the legislature. It is the legislature that determines and expresses the will of the people. Hence, democracy requires that the legislature be obeyed. If it is not, the people do not rule. When the legislature rules a community of any size, it cannot rule directly. Legislatures rule by passing laws, making policy, and hiring people who will carry out their will. In short, legislatures rule by creating bureaucracies! Public bureaucracies are institutions that give expression to the sovereignty of the legislature, and the fundamental duty of members of the bureaucracy is to carry out the will of the legislature.

If so, there is something suspicious about arguments that contrast hierarchy and bureaucracy with democracy. Good democratic citizens may object that decisions that are democratically made are nevertheless unwise. There is, however, something undemocratic in asserting that the legislature need not be obeyed when it is wrong. This same conclusion follows for the legitimate decisions of those functionaries who are hired to do the will of the legislature. School leaders are such functionaries. They are bound by a duty to obey the legitimate decisions of the legislature. They behave democratically when they faithfully carry out the will of the legislature, and they behave undemocratically when they substitute their views for its views. The formal authority of school leaders is gained from their role as servants of the legislature. Their authority is democratic authority.

Third, the arguments that juxtapose democracy and bureaucracy are those of democratic localism and participatory democracy. These arguments seek local governance with significant local deliberation and the pursuit of consensus. Democratic localism requires flat organizations with distributed authority and few externally imposed rules. When we want leaders to be democratic leaders, it seems that we are advocating democratic localism for schools. However, if this view is understood so as to challenge the sovereignty of the legislature, it is simply a mistake. Local schools are not participatory democracies. They are public agencies over whom the legislature is sovereign.

Finally, and importantly, these arguments do not require us to disavow the values of democratic localism in favor of those of representative democracy. What they require is that we express these values in a way that does not challenge the sovereignty of the legislature. We may do this if we view the kind of localism and deliberations that participatory democracy requires as an expression of delegated authority.

That the legislature is sovereign does not require it to govern schools in the minutest detail. Moreover, there are many reasons why legislatures should not seek to do so. Remote legislatures may not understand local needs or conditions. Local decisions may be and often are better decisions.

Moreover, it may be that when decisions are made locally, those who must carry them out will take more responsibility for them and carry them out with more dedication and competence. Many educational scholars (see Chubb & Moe, 1990; Edmonds, 1979) have argued that some measure of autonomy at the building level is a condition of effective schools.

We need a more complex view of democratic leaders. Such leaders must respect the sovereignty of the legislature. They must faithfully seek to carry out the legitimate orders of the legislature, and they must regard themselves as conduits for the authority of the legislature. However, democratic leaders may also attempt to create deliberative and participatory institutions within their schools for teachers and parents. Moreover, they may attempt to persuade the legislature to honor these institutions and respect the decisions they reach.

Hence, I am not suggesting that school leaders stop consulting their teachers or talking with parents and instead start to function like mindless conduits of legislative authority. Indeed, I will soon suggest quite the opposite. I am reminding you that in our society, the legislature is sovereign. If you want the values of democratic localism to reign in your school, you will have to work to create space for these values to operate. That space must continue to respect the sovereignty of the legislature and your duties as an employee of the legislature. Your task is to be a mindful conduit of legislative authority.

PROFESSIONAL COMMUNITY

There is more to be said. Early in this chapter, I expanded our initial scenario by imagining two somewhat intemperate letters that contested the board's decisions and demanded that you oppose them. Each of these letters made arguments that link norms of legitimate authority with conceptions of the nature of a school community and accountability. We need to consider these arguments.

There are hints in the teachers' letter that the teachers are appealing to the norms of democratic localism. They have noted that there has been much deliberation, that parents have been invited to participate, and that they have worked toward consensus. They have pointed to your leadership in these deliberations and referred to you as a democratic leader.

Nevertheless, the core appeal of the teachers' arguments is not to the norms of democratic localism. There are two clues. The first is that the teachers have justified their right to make demands on you by appealing to their expertise. They have not quite said that you should be bound by their decision because it has been democratically achieved. Instead, they are claiming that you should be bound by their view because they are in the best position to make an informed decision and because their primary duty (and *yours*) is to the welfare of the children under their care.

The second clue is that their remarks view students and parents more as clients than as members of a democratic community. This is most clearly the case with respect to students. The teachers have argued that their primary duty is to *serve* their students well. Moreover, the teachers do not claim to have engaged in a deliberation with parents in which parents were viewed as equal participants with them. They claim to have *consulted* with parents and to have taken their views into account.

The norms that teachers are asserting here are those of professionalism, not of participatory democracy. Among the central norms of professionalism are (1) that authority is warranted primarily by expertise, and (2) an ethic of client welfare. Note that these norms are undemocratic. Government is neither of the people nor by the people. Government is of and by "those who know."

A body of professional knowledge is not simply a set of rules that prescribes particular actions under given circumstances. If this were all professional knowledge were, teachers would have no reason to consult and deliberate with one another except, perhaps, to convey something one teacher knows to another who does not. Instead, professional knowledge in education consists of a body of ideas, theories, and collective experience about practice that may shape practice but does not dictate it in detail.

Moreover, in education, professional knowledge is often contradictory and unclear as to how it might be applied. One cannot simply deduce best practice from professional knowledge as though such knowledge were a recipe in a cookbook or a theorem in geometry. Professional knowledge about education must be discussed and debated in order to be applied.

Deliberation is essential to the application of professional knowledge. Deliberation turns knowledge into practice by permitting insights to be pooled; ideas to be criticized, refined, and improved; experience to be shared; and, perhaps most important, local conditions and experience to be taken into account and local problems solved. In education, knowledge and experience are more likely to shed light, add perspective, and suggest possibilities than they are to provide explicit rules of practice that may simply be learned and applied. Judgment is required to connect such knowledge to practice, and judgment is refined by discussion. Professionalism requires collegiality.

Professionalism also requires a collective and collegial concern for the welfare of students. We need to be careful about how we understand the notion of client welfare. Suppose one were to argue, "I am a math teacher. My responsibility is to teach my students mathematics. I am not a baby-sitter or a counselor. Just as the professional responsibility of lawyers to their clients is discharged when they are given proper legal advice and represented competently, my professional responsibility to my students is discharged when I have competently taught them mathematics." Here the idea of a client-centered ethic narrows the obligation to care for students to the obligation to teach them academic subjects.

This position unreasonably truncates the responsibilities of educators for students. Educating students means to care broadly for their growth, not just as students of subject matter but as citizens and human beings. While this is a responsibility that is shared with parents and the community, the responsibility of educators extends to these areas. Moreover, we cannot expect to succeed in educating children and adolescents even in academic subject matters if we do not care for them and about them more broadly. Students need to feel supported and valued if they are to learn. They must have a sense of belonging in the class and the school.

The point can be put in this way. Educators represent three different groups as a part of their professional role: They represent *intellectual communities* and have the responsibility to provide competent instruction in their subject matter. They represent the *citizens of a liberal democratic society* and have the responsibility to create democratic citizens. And they represent *parents and the community* and have the duty to provide nurturance and care for their children. These are intertwined roles, and performing each well enables the accomplishment of all. Hence, we need an expansive view of the requirements of a client-centered ethic. Its essence is not to restrict educators to the narrow role of subject-matter purveyor: It is to urge educators to internalize the broad role of care for their students.

Since professional knowledge is best developed and transformed into practice when collectively shared and deliberated about, it is desirable that educators function as members of professional communities. What are the features of such a community? I would suggest that such communities should be characterized by the following four features:

1. *Professionals must function as colleagues.* This means that they should think of themselves as people engaged in a collective task of educating children. They regularly cooperate with and learn from one another in accomplishing this task.

2. *Professionals must uphold professional standards.* While the collegial interactions of professionals have some of the features of democratic localism, their deliberations are not, at their core, democratic deliberations, and the norms appealed to by professionalism are not democratic norms. Professionals do not claim authority for their decisions because their decisions are democratically achieved. They claim authority for their decisions because they possess expertise that others do not that is required for competent practice.

3. *Trust and respect are easier when a professional community is cooperating together in working toward shared ends that are rooted in professional standards and a client-centered ethic.* In professional communities, people may disagree about the nature of best practice, and disagreements may occasionally be sharp and deeply felt. Nevertheless, it is easier to trust and respect those with whom one disagrees when it is clear that the disagreement is about the best way to achieve shared ends than when disagreement is rooted in competition for scarce resources for achieving one's own interests.

4. *School leaders in schools that have become professional communities might be thought of as "first among equals."* Authority in professional communities should flow from the power of the better argument. It should not be a function of position or power. If the view of the leader is to prevail, it must be because the leader has the better argument rather than because the leader is in a position to enforce his or her will. The primary role of leader in a professional learning community is to create and maintain a climate where professional norms are respected and the power of the better argument prevails.

What does accountability look like in a professional learning community? Accountability is essentially to the professional norms of the group and to the members of the community who share these norms. Professionalism is not merely an individual matter. Norms are taught, maintained, and modified through the collective discussion and practice of professionals. Hence, to behave as a professional is not only to have internalized the norms of the profession and to be competent in one's practice; it is to participate in the deliberations of the community and to respect its collective judgments. It is to be a part of a certain form of culture with its own norms and practices.

Professionals are accountable to one another as well as to internalized principles. They have the dual responsibility to contribute to the deliberations of the community and to consider the views of other professionals. Occasionally professionals have the unpleasant duty to discipline other professionals. While teachers are not, as a rule, legally entitled to render official judgments about their colleagues, nevertheless, if professional communities are to function well, educators must accept responsibility for creating and maintaining a culture where professional behavior is expected and unprofessional behavior is discouraged.

What I have argued in this section of this chapter might seem inconsistent with what I claimed about democracy in the first section (see Strike, 1990b). There I claimed that the primary obligation of school leaders in a democratic society was to respect the sovereignty of the legislature. In this section I have claimed that professionalism does not appeal either to the norms of representative democracy or to the norms of democratic localism. Instead, the central norm of professionalism is "those who know should rule," a norm that I described as undemocratic. Yet I have spoken positively about professionalism, urged educators to think of themselves as professional colleagues, and claimed that school leaders have a responsibility to create professional communities in their schools. These claims might seem inconsistent.

They are not. In democratic societies, school leaders must respect the sovereignty of the legislature. Moreover, the sovereignty of the legislature trumps professionalism. Hence, the teachers of your school are wrong if they claim that you have an obligation to disobey your school board and to act on their views rather than on the policies of the school board. Nevertheless, the wise legislature will recognize the importance of professional communities and will refrain from micromanaging educational practice. Indeed, on my view, the wise legislature will act to encourage professional communities and cede considerable authority to them, and school leaders will do what is in their power not only to create such communities in their schools but to seek space for them to operate.

LOCAL COMMUNITY AND PARENTAL AUTHORITY

What shall we say about the arguments made in the parents' letter? Two arguments are implicit in their letter. First, they claim that their authority over the education of their children trumps the authority of the school. It is their view that you need their permission concerning how to educate their children. Second, they view themselves as a kind of democratic community, a participatory democratic polity whose decisions are binding on you because they represent the considered will of the community.

Each of these arguments has some merit, but ultimately neither can be sustained. Our society tends to view the education of children as a kind of shared project between the family and the state (Gutmann, 1987), in which both parents and schools have a role and a certain authority. While parents must send their children to school, they need not send their children to a public school. A Supreme Court case, *Pierce v. Society of Sisters* (1925), recognized two basic principles: (1) While parents may be required to educate their children, they may not be required to send their children to a public school; and (2) governments may regulate all schools, public and private, with respect to the public interest.

Often courts or legislatures have recognized parental authority over the education of their own children by permitting some exemption from public education. *Wisconsin v. Yoder* (1972) exempts the Amish from compulsory education after elementary school. In most states, parents may also educate their children at home with some public supervision. Many of these exemptions are intended to permit parents to have greater influence over the religious or moral education of their children. They recognize the authority of parents.

At the same time, state governments have wide authority to regulate not only public but private education. Moreover, once parents elect to send their children to a public school, parents are not given very much say concerning the education their children receive. Parents may receive exemptions from some activities for religious reasons. *West Virginia v. Barnette* (1943) exempts religious objectors from compulsory flag salutes and the Pledge of Allegiance. However, so long as public schools do not coerce belief or practice, courts have not been willing to grant parents the right to exempt their children from parts of the curriculum they find objectionable, even if the objections are religiously motivated (see *Mozart v. Hawkins County Public Schools*, 1986). Nor have parents been given any right to demand that their child receive different instruction from what is made available to other children.

These policies express three commitments. First, the authority of parents to oversee the education of their children is protected by granting them a right to choose a private school for their child as well as by their right to function as citizens in democratic elections for those representatives who govern education. Second, there is a weighty public interest in education that warrants the right of government to regulate education, to make provision for education through public schools, and to determine the content of that education. Finally, the practicalities of the matter weigh heavily against ceding to parents the right to determine the nature of the education of their children in detail once they have chosen a public school for them. It is hard to see how schools could offer a coherent education at all if parents had broad rights to demand exemptions or special curricula for their children.

In short, our society, quite sensibly, views the education of its children as a shared project between parents and the state, recognizing that parents and the community have legitimate interests in the education of children. This shared authority has been worked out in such a way that parents have not been ceded significant authority over the details of the education of their children in public schools.

Hence, the parents in our case are wrong insofar as they claim that you have a legal duty or a moral obligation to do what they want when their demands conflict either with the demands of the legislature or with the necessities of providing a competent education. The legislature, not parents, is sovereign over education once children appear in a public school. You are not accountable (in this way) to the parents in your school for the manner in which their children are educated.

These points are, however, points about the rights of parents to control the education of their children and about various legal conceptions and policies that influence these rights. Nothing here prevents sensible school leaders of public schools from listening to parents, respecting their views, and taking their desires and requests into account. Moreover, there are many reasons why leaders should do this.

Once it is disconnected from claims about rights and legal authority, the argument of the parents has a point. These children are their children. They are, in a sense, on loan to the school. Parents may be presumed (usually) to have the best interest of their children at heart and unique insight into what their children's interests are. Moreover, when parents feel respected, listened to, and when their views and requests are taken seriously, they are more likely to support the school and its efforts and programs. School leaders who respect parents build an educational asset for their schools.

These remarks have considered the right of parents as individuals. However, the parents of our school also have claimed authority as a collectivity. We might ascribe two central claims to them. First, the parents (perhaps along with the teachers, students, and other members of the local community) claim to be a kind of polity, a political community. Second, they claim to be the primary political community so far as the governance of any given school is concerned. Thus, when there is conflict between their views and the views of other political jurisdictions, their views should prevail.

In support of this view, these parents might claim the support of the arguments for democratic localism. Democracy works best when it is local and deliberative. When polities are small and deliberative, arguments are more likely to focus on the common good of the citizens of the community, the power of the better argument is more likely to prevail, and ownership of decisions and cooperation in shared projects may be greater.

We can make several points in favor of these arguments. First, while the families whose children attend a given school are not the only ones who are affected by the education provided, they are those who are primarily affected. If power over decisions or institutions ought to be proportional to the extent that those decisions or institutions have consequences for people, then these families should have considerable influence over the schools their children attend.

Second, localism in decision making may increase participation and involvement. It may also increase what has been called *intergeneration closure* (see Coleman & Hoffer, 1987). When parents are deeply involved in the schools their children attend, they may come to know and consider the needs of other children and become involved in their lives. Participation may increase the competence of participants, who will come to know the problems of their schools better and have more realistic views on how to solve them. Local participatory democracies can build what has been called social capital and make it available to children.

There are cases where schools have been organized as local and participatory democracies with some (varying) degrees of success (see Apple & Beane, 1995). Some private and alternative public schools have institutionalized significant roles in school governance for parents and sometimes students. Schools developed by the Society of Friends often do this. Some alternative and charter schools have institutionalized the all-school meeting where parents, teachers, and students meet and make certain kinds of decisions.

Some larger jurisdictions have created institutions for parental and community participation. The Chicago school reform legislation of 1986 (see Bryk, Sebring, Kerbow, Rollow, & Easton, 1998) created school councils with considerable power for each Chicago public school. New York has required each school district to create mechanisms for parental and community participation, although these groups were rarely given anything particularly important to do.

There are numerous difficulties with such arrangements. If parents and community members are to play a significant role in school governance, these roles must be institutionalized and codified. It must be clear who has the authority to decide what, and how people obtain the roles and authority they are to exercise. Ad hoc collections of parents cannot simply declare themselves to have authority over self-selected matters. When institutions of local democracy are added to a large and complex governance system, as was the case in Chicago, the result can be confusion and gridlock more than the empowerment of parents and community members because the decision-making system becomes more complex and lines of authority less clear.

Another concern is that local participatory democracies require interest, time, and talent. They can become government by the committed, government by those with significant leisure, or government by the articulate. Sometimes time and talent are differentially available along class lines so that the institutions of participatory democracy can become infected with class bias.

The fundamental problem with the arguments that have been suggested here by your school's parents is that they have been expressed as a claim about sovereignty. These parents have argued that they have a right to be the primary decision-makers concerning the school that educates their children. They have said that you, the principal, are accountable primarily to them and have implied that their views trump those of the school board and the state legislature. They do not. The fundamental expression of democracy in our society is the commitment to the sovereignty of the legislature. Here the relevant legislatures are the school board and the state legislature. To respect democracy is to recognize their sovereignty over education in their jurisdictions.

Nothing in this argument, however, prevents legislatures from ceding some of their decision-making authority to local institutions, and nothing in the argument prevents you from creating participatory practices for teachers and parents within the space provided by the legislature. Moreover, the arguments I have developed here strongly suggest that this is a good thing to do. Schools are best served by respecting and considering the professional judgment of teachers and by encouraging the participation of parents and community members.

This last point can be put as one about community. A sense of community is created when common purpose is created through participation. Everyone benefits when teachers, parents, community members, and students view the school as *their* school, when they see themselves as members of a school community. The task of the school leader, then, is to seek to create community by empowering professional judgment and local deliberation within the spaces provided by representative democracy and to expand these spaces where possible.

This will make your life more complicated. It will tend to disperse authority among different individuals and groups. It will generate role conflicts for you as you try to honor the sovereignty of the legislature while also respecting the collective professional judgment of your teachers and the voice of parents. However, mastering these tensions will also create a better school.

ACCOUNTABILITY

In this chapter, we have discussed a number of principles that can be appealed to in order to justify authority and legitimate decisions. Let me list them briefly as aphorisms about how decisions are legitimated:

- *Representative democracy:* Decisions are legitimate when they are made by a properly elected legislature.
- *Individualism:* Decisions are legitimate when they express the choices of individuals or are consistent with the rights of individuals.
- *Professionalism:* Decisions are legitimate when they are made as the result of the deliberations of those who have the knowledge and

experience to make them well and are in the interest of those for
whom they are made.
- *Democratic localism:* Decisions are legitimate when they are the product
of the deliberations of those whom they immediately affect.

These legitimization principles can be used to help us understand
accountability. Because so much emphasis has been put on standards and
on testing right now in the United States, we tend to think of accountability largely as a matter of meeting benchmarks for achievement that are
defined by test scores. *NCLB* also makes schools accountable for reducing
achievement gaps by insisting that test scores be disaggregated by race
and socioeconomic status and that schools get the achievement of all
groups above specified benchmarks.

The political principles I have just specified will permit us a broader
view of what is possible. Consider several ways we might answer the "to
whom" question about accountability:

1. *To the legislature:* As noted, currently the "to whom" of accountability
   is to the legislature.

2. *To parents:* We are not merely a democratic society, we are a liberal
   and a capitalist society with a market economy. Liberal societies
   must respect the rights of individuals. Our society claims that
   parents have some right to oversee the education of their children,
   especially when it comes to the values or religious convictions that
   permeate the education they receive. This right is largely protected
   in our society by the right to select a private school for one's children.

3. *To professional standards and the professional community:* Another response
   to the "to whom" question is that schools should be accountable to
   the professional community and to its standards. The practical
   import of this idea is that the professional staff of a school should
   deliberate about the nature and quality of the education that they
   are providing and make judgments about these matters according to
   their professional standards.

4. *To the school's community:* A final response to the "to whom" question
   is that educators are accountable to their students, their student's
   parents, and the community that is most directly involved and
   affected by the local school. Your school's parents may be wrong in
   their claim that their collective views should be taken as the highest
   authority about how their children are educated, but they are certainly right about the claim that these children are their children;
   that schools exist, first and foremost, to serve them; and that, as a
   consequence, they should be heard and attended to. Parents, especially, need to be informed and listened to. They need to understand

but also to help shape the aspirations of the schools their children attend. Moreover, when schools have a sense of themselves as accountable to parents, they are likely to find that they come to better understand the needs of their students and the community in which they live. Good education cannot occur without such an understanding.

Which of these views should prevail? The argument of this chapter suggests two conclusions: First, when these different visions of accountability conflict, the sovereignty of the legislature takes precedence. Second, a fully responsible view of accountability will take all of these principles into account. The school leader, therefore, is responsible not only to obey the legislature, but also to create institutions that respect the professional judgment of teachers and the voice of parents, both as individuals speaking for their own children and as a collective speaking for the school community.

One benefit of such a balanced view of accountability is that it helps to put the role of tests in accountability into perspective. Test results are commonly employed to generate benchmarks that educators are expected to meet. This is the core of *NCLB*. Educators are expected to meet Annual Yearly Proficiency goals that are specified in terms of the percentages of students who are proficient as defined by their states.

Standards and testing may, however, abet other forms of accountability. Public reports of test results may function to make schools more accountable to parents and community members. And test results may be a form of consumer information when parents seek to select a school for their children. However, it is the legislature that determines what is tested for, creates or purchases tests, mandates when and to whom they are given, defines success and failure, specifies how results are reported, and attaches rewards and punishments to results. Here, fundamentally, accountability is to the legislature.

Might not test results also contribute to the deliberations of professionals, and, thereby, to the development of a professional culture that takes the use of data in decision making seriously? Of course. (I will discuss this more fully in the next chapter.) But an excessive relying on test results misses much of the real import of professional accountability. The crucial thing that professionals must do is to use test data to determine whether a collectively achieved and praiseworthy conception of education has been achieved, and, if it has not been adequately achieved, what to do about this. This goal is not achieved if test results become the meaning of a good education rather than merely one measure of whether a good education has been achieved.

There is much that we need to know that we will not learn from test scores. Consider language instruction. What are we likely to get test data about? We might expect tests to tell us how well our students can read. We might also expect useful data about how well they can write. For secondary students, reasonable tests might be constructed to measure the grasp of certain things about literature. But tests are unlikely to tell us if a student loves Shakespeare or Morrison. Tests may tell us if students can write well-structured essays, but they are unlikely to reveal whether they can write with elegance, style, or grace, or whether they can write good poems or construct persuasive arguments.

This is not just a point about allegedly subjective areas such as literature. It is also the case that tests are unlikely to tell us if students have learned to take a scientific outlook toward the world, whether they are committed to the importance of rigor and consistency in mathematics, whether they have learned to experience the elegance of a powerful proof, whether they find nature a source of awe or beauty, or whether they can appreciate a well-executed fast break.

There is a great deal about what constitutes a good education that schools will not be held accountable for if the only form of accountability is accountability to the legislature for meeting benchmarks defined by test scores. Many aspects of the appreciation and deep understanding of various subject matters will be missed. We will not attend greatly to citizenship. Nor will we pay close attention to other than the basic academic needs of students. These things are not likely to be attended to unless they are upheld in the conversations and deliberations of leaders and teachers who will be concerned for them because their professional knowledge and a client-centered ethic evoke such concerns.

Note that this discussion of the role of professional knowledge suggests a weakness in the formulation of the division of labor between the legislature and the educational professionals who staff the school suggested in the quote that began this chapter. There, the author suggests that the state will determine the *what* and educators will determine the *how*. This formulation suggests that the professional expertise of educators largely concerns the techniques of teaching. Hopefully, teachers do possess knowledge of pedagogy. But it is also to be hoped that teachers will have a deep grasp of those forms of understanding that inhere in subject matter and of how what is taught in schools can contribute to the enrichment of life. These things are unlikely to be well captured in standards and are even less likely to be captured in tests. Yet an understanding of these things shapes pedagogy. How we teach and what we expect to accomplish in teaching are not separate matters.

A full-blooded and multifaceted view of accountability is, thus, a requirement of a full-blooded and multifaceted view of a good education. We attend to test results because the legislature insists that we do so and because tests can provide useful data to aid our decision making. But we listen to teachers because they are the ones most likely to have a rich view of their subjects and a well-rounded vision of a good education. And we listen to parents because they have a deep concern for the welfare of their children over a wide range of concerns. If we are only accountable to the legislature for test scores, we will truncate the education we provide. If we are also accountable to professional standards, professional teachers, and parents, we will have a wider range of information about a richer view of education.

CONCLUSIONS

The arguments of this chapter can be summed up in two broad ideas. First, there are multiple norms of legitimate authority in our society. The sovereignty of the legislature must be respected, as must individual rights. Expertise must be respected. The voices of those most immediately affected by our institutions and practices must be heard and considered. Second, schools and school leaders should be informed by a vision of accountability that takes into account all of these multiple norms. Schools and leaders are accountable to the legislature, to their teachers when they speak as professionals, and to students, parents, and the local community. No one form of accountability is adequate. If we think of accountability only as meeting prescribed benchmarks, the education we provide will be distorted, as it will be if we overemphasize any of the forms of authority and accountability I have discussed.

To be sure, this view of authority and accountability will make the lives of school leaders complicated. They will be beset with conflicting demands and expectations. Many of these demands and expectations will carry some authority. Schools leaders should view themselves as intermediaries and as community builders. Intermediaries present the claims of one party to other parties faithfully and press for their fair considerations. Community builders create institutions and practices in which, despite disagreement, people share common purpose, seek the common good, and solve their problems and disputes by open and respectful discussion informed by relevant evidence. Perhaps the best definition of a democratic leadership is that it consists of the will and ability to do these things.

6

Ethical Decision Making

Growth is the only evidence of life.

—John Henry Newman (Bartlett, 1955)

The brightest flashes in the world of thought are incomplete until they have been proven to have their counterparts in the world of fact.

—John Tyndall (Bartlett, 1955)

PROLOGUE AND SCENARIO

In this chapter, I discuss the ethics of decision making. Chapter 5 was partly about this. It concerned one aspect of legitimate decision making: who has authority over decisions. As we shall see below, there are other aspects of legitimate decision making. Some of them concern the proper use of evidence.

Leaders are frequently urged to employ data-driven decision making. I will argue that rather than thinking of decisions as data-driven, we should think of them as evidence-driven. The point is to recognize a wider range of what counts as evidence than test scores and to encourage professional community. In what follows, I also want to discuss due process. Due process concerns the proper use of evidence. I will argue that we should think of the rules of due process as a kind of institutionalized rationality. To discuss these issues, I will begin with two connected scenarios. Suppose now that the school introduced in the first chapter is a high school, and you are its principal. Suppose also that while it is usually true that your students do well on state tests, there are some exceptions. History is one of them.

Your state has a test in history that all students must take and pass if they are to graduate. Moreover, your state has benchmarks for your school to achieve concerning the percentage of students who pass this exam.

Your school has a significant percentage of African American students. As a consequence, your history curriculum places considerable emphasis on African American history. At the same time, your school is located in a largely middle-class neighborhood. While your students are racially diverse, their parents are reasonably affluent, and there are no great disparities between the family incomes of students of different races.

You obtain data from the state about how many of your students have passed the history test, as well as a breakdown of this data by race, gender, and socioeconomic status (SES). The data tell you two important things: First, the percentage of students who are passing this test is below the state's benchmarks. Second, there are no significant differences between races on the test. You get together with your faculty to discuss these results. What is the relevance of these data to your decision making about your program?

Daniel Wilkins is a nontenured history teacher in your school. Next year a decision about his tenure will have to be made. While the procedures for deciding tenure are complex, and any decision must be approved by your district's superintendent and voted on by the board of education, nevertheless, the decision is really yours. You do the evaluations, and you make the recommendations. These recommendations are almost always followed.

You are not happy with Daniel. Nor are the other members of his department. While there is a lot to say about his teaching, some good and some not so good, two things stand out. First, he does not agree with the educational program your staff has worked so hard to develop. In the many meetings that were held while the program was being developed, he argued for a different curriculum, one that placed less emphasis on African American history and emphasized more traditional teaching methods. He continues to make these arguments. In the meetings to discuss the board of education's new requirements, he was the only teacher to support them. Now that students have not done as well as hoped on the state tests, he feels vindicated. Because he is there, meetings are longer, more acrimonious, and less productive. He is frequently the holdout from what would otherwise be a consensus. He is not combative about this, but he is persistent, and he is not on the same page with the other teachers. Second, he has not followed the program that has been developed. He goes into his classroom, shuts the door, and does what he wants. You know this because parents have complained. When you show up for official evaluation sessions, he tries to show you what he thinks you want to see.

It is unclear how effective he is in the classroom. Part of the evidence you have concerning the achievement of his students comes from the state tests, which allow you to look at results for each classroom. Daniel's students appear to score as well on these tests as students of other teachers do. However, you are not supposed to use these data to evaluate teachers, and you agree that you should not. These tests are not suitable for this purpose. Nevertheless, you suppose that some of your teachers would argue that Daniel's students succeed on the tests because he teaches to the tests, whereas they do not. And since he pays little attention to African American history, they would question whether he is effective in meeting the goals they have set for their history program.

Decision making can be painful and difficult. Some decisions are contentious. You may find that some of your staff or parents don't support you. Most decisions have consequences for other people. These consequences can be serious, even devastating to them. Decisions about discipline or employment can be like this. Sometimes you must recommend the expulsion of a student or the nonrenewal or termination of a teacher. No decent person can take pleasure in excluding a student or terminating an employee. Sometimes any decision you make seems to harm someone. It's nice to have win-win choices, but the world often doesn't give them to you.

Your decisions are often subject to challenge. People may claim that you are wrong: Your decisions are unwise and based on faulty argument, false premises, or the wrong values. The legitimacy of your decisions can be challenged, regardless of whether they are right or wrong: You are not entitled to make this decision. You did not follow the proper procedures. You did not consult the right people. Your decision is in some way illegal. What is a good decision? How are good decision made?

In what follows, I will take on three tasks. First, I will develop a model of good decision making that I will use to provide a kind of overview of ethical decision making. Second, I will discuss some issues concerned with evidence-based decision making and the ethics of means-ends reasoning. Third, I will discuss due process.

THE ANATOMY OF ETHICAL DECISION MAKING

In my preliminary comments, I have noted several different aspects of good decisions. The following definition attends to these features: A good decision is one that has four characteristics.

1. The decision is supported by evidence. This evidence supports the claim that acting on this decision is more likely to achieve desired ends at an appropriate cost than other courses of action that might be taken.

2. The ends aimed at by the decision are the ends that ought to be aimed at.

3. The decision can be implemented morally.

4. The decision has been legitimately achieved.

Let's consider some features of this definition. Parts 1 and 2 of the definition suggest that at its core, decision making involves ends-means reasoning. One specifies the ends desired. Then one finds the most efficient or most cost-effective means of pursuing these ends. There are, to be sure, caveats and complexities here, but ends-means reasoning is at the heart of decision making.

While it might seem that there is not much ethical content to ends-means reasoning, that is not true. Part 1 of my definition requires commitment to at least two ethical norms. The first commitment is to evidence-based decisions. The second is to efficiency.

Perhaps these norms seem uncontroversial, but they are often disregarded. People may prefer educational strategies that are comfortable or traditional, regardless of whether they are supported by evidence or are efficient. Even worse, people may prefer decisions that serve their own self–interest, regardless of whether they efficiently serve good ends.

A commitment to evidence-based decision making and efficiency requires other commitments. If we want evidence-based decisions, we must take research and inquiry seriously, learn to be reflective about what counts as evidence, and become competent in assessing evidence.

We must also become serious about deliberation and about becoming a professional community. Good reasoning is a group activity! Hence, these ideas have implications for the kind of school culture you should try to create. And, as I will discuss below, we must become serious about due process since, at its core, due process concerns the appraisal of evidence.

Part 2 of my definition suggests that we have to justify the ends we aim at as well as the means we choose to achieve them. The ends we aim at are the ones we ought to aim at. They must be worthy and legitimate ends. Ultimately, an inquiry about worthy and legitimate ends will take us to the kinds of fundamental questions addressed in Chapters 2 and 3 of this book. What are the basic goals of education? How can we make sure we provide for equal opportunity? It may also take us to the kinds of questions we addressed in Chapter 5. Who is entitled to choose the aims of education—elected officials, parents, or experts?

Part 3 of my definition of good decision making requires us to consider the means we choose not only from a perspective of efficiency, but also from a moral perspective. Consider the popular cliché, the ends do not justify the means. In one sense, this is clearly wrong. How could we justify the means we choose without showing that they served worthy ends?

What this cliché sensibly means might be captured in two ideas. The first is that we are not at liberty to evaluate means *solely* in terms of whether they achieve the ends we have chosen to aim at. Means may have consequences other than the ones we aim at. We need to evaluate all of the consequences for all affected. The second idea is that there may be reasons that indicate that a given decision cannot be morally implemented regardless of the balance of good over bad consequences.

Consider a somewhat flippant example. Suppose you find that some of your students are cheating on tests. You approach this problem by making it clear to students that they are not to cheat, you devise some ways to monitor whether they are cheating, and you prescribe punishments for cheating. How severe should the punishments be? You answer this question by saying to yourself that the punishment must be severe enough to stop cheating. It must convey the message that cheating is unacceptable and provide adequate incentives to ensure that it is not worthwhile for students to cheat.

were you to engage in public summary execution
ould send the message that cheating is not accept-
that few students would be willing to risk sum-
ng. Summary execution would efficiently achieve
t such a policy?
policy does not take all of the consequences into
ting students is, after all, a consequence. It does
and their families. When we consider all of the
of harm done compared to the good achieved is
ost unfavorable. ciple of benefit maximization is not satisfied.

The second reason is that punishment should fit the crime. While it is not always clear how we decide whether a punishment fits the crime, it does seem as though we should not decide this matter entirely by asking such questions as whether the punishment will deter others from similar acts or whether adequate messages are conveyed. Rather, we determine fit by making some assessment of how severe the crime was and what kind of punishment a crime of this severity deserves. There is a moral norm of proportionality about punishment that we should follow and that does not depend on the consequences of punishment.

A more serious example: Suppose that you decide not to recommend Daniel Wilkins for tenure. You make this decision employing ends-means reasoning. You are concerned for the educational welfare of the children in your school. You believe that the fact that Daniel is "not with the program" ultimately has deleterious consequences for your students. Moreover, his noncompliance and constant disagreement is eroding the cohesiveness of your faculty. You are not persuaded that he is effective in the classroom, especially given your goals for the history curriculum. You are persuaded that this decision is best for your students and your school.

Can the decision be ethically implemented? First, you must consider all of the (knowable) consequences of the action. The action may harm Daniel and his family. It may affect the morale of your teachers. While Daniel may not be with the program, it may be that you will be unable to replace him with someone who is as able as he. Thus, there are other matters to consider, some of which also affect your school and have consequences that go beyond its boundaries.

You might also need to consider other factors. You will need to justify your decision to the school board. It has occurred to you that the school board is not exactly on board with your program, either. Indeed, the requirements they have recently imposed on the district seem reasonably consistent with the way that Daniel teaches. You are not eager to write the board a report that they might interpret as saying that you are not renewing Daniel's contract because he agrees with the board rather than with you and your teachers. You will have to write a report than covers up this little dilemma, and you may have to invent other reasons for your decision.

Suppose you have to defend these reasons. That should not be too much of a problem. Daniel does not have tenure. He has no right to demand a hearing or to require you to defend your decision. So long as you say the right things to the board and to him, you are home free. But you will have to bend the truth a little. You are beginning to sacrifice your integrity to succeed in pursuing a decision that you believe is a good one, but which you cannot publicly defend. This is something you should not be willing to do.

In short, while you have some reasons to believe that recommending that Daniel not have his contract renewed will make your school a better school, it is not clear that overall the consequences of this action do more good than harm. Moreover, you are not sure that you can do what would be required without sacrificing your integrity. If this is the case, perhaps you should consider a different approach to the problem—one that not only produces good outcomes for your school, but which you can implement in an ethical way. Discussing your view of his performance with him might be a good place to start.

We now have an agenda for thinking about the ethics of decision-making. First, I want to consider the ethical aspect of ends-means reasoning, focusing on the ethics of evidence-based decision making. Second, I want to consider some "procedural" aspects of ethical decision making. Good decisions should respect due process, be open and transparent, and be made in a way that avoids conflicts of interest.

ENDS-MEANS REASONING AND EVIDENCE-BASED DECISION MAKING: CHOOSING ENDS

The standards movement involves more than a view of accountability. It is also a view about decision making. The basic story line goes like this. Rational decisions employ effective means to chosen ends. If we want to be rational about education or anything else, then we need first to select the ends we wish to pursue. Then we need to select means that will realize these ends. How are we to do these things?

How are we to select ends? The standards movement has not been very clear about this, and, it turns out, this is a complex matter. I want to discuss two mistaken ideas that have occasionally been put forth. The first idea is that we can be rational only about the means we select to pursue our goals, but we cannot be rational about the ends we pursue. The second idea is that goals must be measurable.

The first view (Ayer, 1946) begins with the claim that we can only have knowledge of two kinds. First, we can know mathematical truths and other claims that are true by definition. While claims such as "$2 + 2 = 4$" do not describe anything we can empirically verify, we can know that such claims are true because they are what philosophers call *tautologies*, claims that are true by definition. Just as the claim that "all unicorns have one horn" is true in virtue of what we mean by *unicorn* (even though there are none), "2 + 2 = 4" is true because of what we mean by 2, +, =, and 4. Second, we can know scientific claims. Ultimately, scientific claims are those that can be verified through our senses.

Other claims, this view holds, are not verifiable in one of these ways. Therefore, they cannot be decided by reason and may be meaningless. Claims about values, this view holds, cannot be verified and might best be viewed as expressions of feelings or emotions rather than as claims about what is true or reasonable. "Murder is wrong" means "I don't like murder" or "phooey on murder."

This view can be expanded into a view of decision making by arguing that, while we cannot decide rationally whether what we want is what we ought to want, we can nevertheless discover what it is that we collectively want. Indeed, some argue, this is what democracy is about. We cannot all have everything we want. As economists are alleged to say, "Wants are infinite, resources are finite." Since we cannot all have all of what we want, the trick is to ensure that as many of us get as much of what we want as is possible.

Democracy (more or less) does this. Politicians, if they are to get elected, must get a majority of the votes. To do this, they must persuade a majority of voters that they will get more of what they want if they vote for them rather than another candidate. They do this by "packaging wants," that is, finding out what people want and proposing policies that they hope will be seen by a majority of voters as likely to deliver on wants better than the opposing candidate's policies would. In a legislature, representatives must do something similar if they are able to get legislation passed. What democratic politics does is to vector interests.

Once it is known what most people want, we can make rational and scientific choices about the means that are likely to succeed in producing what democratic politics has determined are desirable outcomes. Now we have a view of decision making. We choose ends democratically and means scientifically.

This picture of decision making is flawed for many reasons. Unfortunately, it is difficult to pursue the complex debates required to argue these points in what is intended as a brief chapter in a short book. But two comments may give you some notion of how problematic these ideas are. Consider this claim: "The only ideas that we can know to be true are tautologies or those we can verify with our senses." How do we know this is true? It is not a tautology. Neither does it seem that we can verify it through our senses. Hence, the view of knowledge underlying this conception of decision making is not knowable on its own terms.

Or consider the idea that democracy vectors interests allowing us (collectively) to get as much of what we want as is possible. This view seems to assume two other ideas. One is the idea that justice consists in the greatest good for the greatest number. It is the social application of the principle of benefit maximization. The second is that, other things being equal, each of us has the same right to have our wants satisfied as anyone else.

These claims are moral norms. If they are just unverifiable subjective preferences, then why should they carry any more weight in decision-making than the idea, for example, that you should get what you want only after all of my wants are fully satisfied? "That is unjust!" you argue. But that is just your subjective opinion. Why should I care? The idea that we cannot make a rational selection of values, we can only choose them, leads to significant contradictions and itself makes value assumptions.

Consider how many states actually went about developing content standards under a previous federal program, *Goals 2000*. The various processes employed involved consultation with subject matter experts and teachers. Public hearings were held. Debates were engaged in. Legislatures provided funding and vetted reports. Stakeholders were involved. Various questions were addressed, such as, What kinds of knowledge and skills are valuable for what reasons? The reasons discussed ranged from the requirements of a modern economy to the requirements of a constitutional liberal democracy. They included epistemological questions, What is the best understanding we have of this domain of ideas? and What is inquiry like in this area? And there were questions concerned with legitimation: Who are the stakeholders that are entitled to a say?

These are not the kinds of processes we would adopt and questions that we would ask if we believed that the various ends we seek in education were largely matters of subjective choice beyond the grasp of reason. They are processes and questions that assume that there are many different questions to debate and to answer.

We must debate what is valuable. We must understand the nature of various subject matters. We must consider the nature of the society we want. We must know who is entitled to a say and to decide. Nothing here is easy, but nothing is merely a matter of subjective preference beyond the grasp of reason.

MEASURABLE GOALS?

Should our goals be measurable? The argument for this is that unless our ends are measurable, we cannot make a rational selection of means. We cannot do this because the rational selection of means is essentially an empirical matter. We must try something and see if it works. To do this, we need a way to decide if we have achieved the results we have chosen. We cannot do this if our ends cannot be measured.

The argument makes a critical assumption. It is not true that to know if we have achieved some end, we must be able to *measure* it. What is true is that we need a way to *recognize* whether we have achieved our ends. These are not the same thing.

A simple example: I am writing these sentences in my university office. Shortly I will head home. How will I know if I achieve my goal? Well,

I know where my house is and what it looks like. When I open the door, the person who greets me should be my wife. I know what she looks like. All of these things I can observe without measuring anything. Hence, I can recognize whether I have achieved my goal without measuring anything.

Nevertheless, there are some goals that must be measured if we are to decide whether we have attained them. I am now contemplating my retirement. To do this, I have to decide whether I have enough money to retire. To address this question I need numbers and projections. If I send off to TIAA-CREF, who holds my retirement funds, to find out how I'm doing, and they tell me that my situation is not so bad, they will not have told me what I need. I need a precise measure of my assets.

The conclusion to draw is that we need measurable objectives in some cases and not others, and for some purposes and not others. The question is when we need measurable objectives and for what purposes.

In recent years, I have taught philosophy of education and education law. I assign papers. Then I evaluate them. (Note that I did not say that I grade them, although I do that as well.) My evaluations are normally given in the form of written comments, some of which refer to specific places in the paper. At the end there is usually a summative evaluation. The text-specific comments often say things like, "This argument doesn't follow," "You don't understand this legal doctrine," "Good point, but have you considered this," "I see why you want to say this. I disagree. But you've made a good case nevertheless," or "Good argument." My summative comments may say something about the overall argument that has been made, but I usually also try to tell students how their work "measures up" to my standards for their performance. And at some point I transform these comments into a grade—a measure of quality. I do not need to measure anything to provide evaluative comments on these papers, and it is these evaluative comments that are educationally important. It is these comments from which students are most likely to learn.

It is, however, often useful to students to be told how their work "measures up" to some standard which, in the language of testing, may be either norm-referenced (e.g., "About what a bright junior should do") or criterion-referenced (e.g., "If you want to be a lawyer, you'll need to be able to work through arguments like this one"). These comments do provide measures of a kind, although they do not provide measures that are either precise or quantitative. It does not follow that they are bad measures. Indeed, it may be more useful to students who aspire to law school to be told that they are not doing law school–quality work than to tell them that they have gotten an 86.

The measures I provide serve legitimate goals. It is important to students and to the university to know how students are doing. I can tell individual students how they are doing in a loose language: "You are doing about what a bright junior should." I must be a little clearer when I tell the registrar. I have to assign a letter grade. The registrar takes these letters and transforms them into a GPA carried out to 2 decimals. In the process, my relatively nonquantitative recognition of the merits of the work has been transformed into something quite precise.

Precision is not the same thing as accuracy. The process of grading is fraught with peril. I have had students who have received a grade below their expectations argue that my judgment is subjective. My typical response is that there is inevitably some measure of subjectivity in my judgment. If I have given a student a B–, it is quite clear to me that one of my colleagues might well have given the student a B+. At the same time, these judgments are not altogether subjective. Reasons can be given for such grades. It would be unlikely that I would give an A to a paper to which a colleague would give an F.

Occasionally, a student who has struggled with a paper asks for a rubric. What I usually say to this request is that I can describe in broad terms what a good paper is. If it is helpful for me to tell you that a good argument is one whose premises are true and where the conclusion follows from them, I can say things like this. In fact, I have a document entitled "How to Write a Good Paper" that I distribute to every class I teach. Such advice is often unhelpful to students who are struggling with a paper. Yet I cannot do more. One reason is that I cannot anticipate where the student's paper will go. Once I see the argument, I can explain why I think it is reasonable or unreasonable, but I must see it first.

Were I to create rubrics for evaluating papers in advance, they would be problematic in certain ways. For example, they would not anticipate original arguments. I do not deny that I could construct a rubric that would allow me to decide whether a student understood (at a minimal level) the argument of a Supreme Court case. And I could use this rubric to evaluate a paragraph response to a set question. But it is also true that eminent legal scholars argue complex points about Supreme Court arguments. How would one write a rubric for them?

Three conclusions: First, sometimes the quality of a performance can be recognized without measuring it. Second, the more complex a performance is, the more difficult it is to state in advance criteria for its performance that will permit intersubjective agreement among even well-trained raters. Third, the need to measure is often generated by the purposes of an appraisal. If we want to compare many people against a common standard, we will need measures of some sort.

Some kinds of accountability require measures. We cannot create benchmarks for whether a school has met its Adequate Yearly Progress (AYP) goals under *NCLB* without measures. Moreover, the kinds of performances schools are most likely to be held accountable for, basic skills in reading and math, can be measured with plausible accuracy. The claim that we can aim only at measurable goals, however, should be rejected. There are many educational goals that we can recognize but, if we can measure them at all, it is with considerable difficulty, a high risk of distortion, and great cost.

The important practical questions are whether developing measures for our goals is the best way to recognize whether we have achieved them. This is a debate about our purposes, our measurement technologies, and costs and benefits. Perhaps we could find a way to measure the quality of the annual concert of our high school band. We do want to know whether the concert was a good one. Musically literate people can form reasonable opinions about this and convey them. We can recognize very bad performances and very good ones with ease, but we could only construct plausible quantitative measures of these evaluations with considerable difficulty and some arbitrariness. Why would we want to?

The claim that we should employ measurability as a criterion for any goal we decide to aim for is an error, and a dangerous one. It has the potential to distort and truncate our aims. Many worthy educational aims involve performances: writing persuasive essays, playing an instrument, constructing a proof, doing an experiment. These are all performances of a sort. Competent observers can recognize when they have been done well. Discussing them with students is a basic educational task. Measuring them is pointless and distorting.

What we want are goals that we can recognize. And we want to employ means to recognize them that are appropriate to what we wish to recognize and the purposes we have for attempting to recognize when we have succeeded. Sometimes we will want tests that generate measures of performance. Sometimes we will want competent observers to sit down and discuss performances.

Why is this important? Consider two claims that I have now made several times. First, while test results may be useful measures of some educational goals, they are not adequate definitions of the meaning of a good education. There are worthy goals not tested for. Second, there are multiple forms of accountability. There is accountability to the legislature for meeting specified benchmarks, but there is also accountability to parents and to professional standards. To these I want to add a third claim: The meaning of meeting or failing to meet a measured benchmark is not on the surface of the data.

THE MEANING OF MEETING BENCHMARKS

To see this, let us turn to the first part of our scenario. You are the principal of a high school in a large urban area. Your state has a test in history that all students must take and pass if they are to graduate. Moreover, your state has benchmarks for your school to achieve concerning the percentage of students who pass this exam. Your school has a significant percentage of African American students. As a consequence, your history curriculum places considerable emphasis on African American history. At the same time, your school is located in a middle-class neighborhood. While your students are racially diverse, their parents, on average, are reasonably affluent and there are no great disparities between the family incomes of students of different races.

You obtain data from the state about how many of your students have passed its history test and a breakdown of this data by race, gender, and SES. The data tell you two things. First, the percentage of students who are passing this test is below the state's expectations. Second, there are no significant differences between races on the test. You get together with your faculty to discuss these results. Consider a few directions this conversation might take.

One teacher raises this question: "Why do we care about whether our students learn history?" The teacher makes the following argument: "History is important for two reasons. It helps people to become better citizens because it helps them to understand public issues. Also, it helps students understand who they are. It grounds them and orients them in life." The teacher goes on to argue that the students in your school are taught history in a way that links it to citizenship. They are encouraged to do projects researching events that have shaped their communities. Moreover, students are required to write papers on their research. These papers often reveal an emerging concern for public issues and a growing competence in understanding them. The papers also show that many students begin to achieve a degree of self-understanding by coming to understand the forces that shaped their communities and themselves.

A second teacher argues that this approach to history originated with a discussion among parents about the role of history in a mixed-race school. These parents believed that it was important that African American students understand their own history, but also that it was important in constructing a multiracial community that all students understand African American history. Moreover, these parents had argued that part of history instruction should involve projects in which students worked together to understand the forces that had shaped their city. They had been instrumental in persuading the faculty of your school to develop their approach to teaching history. The teacher concludes with this remark: "Not only has this curriculum helped to create a multiracial community in our school, it would be disrespectful to these parents who have trusted us to assist in this endeavor to alter the curriculum without their participation."

A third teacher chimes in: "Our evaluation of student work and our observations of student interactions indicate to us that our approach to history is successful in meeting our goals. At the same time, these data suggest that our students' knowledge of history is spotty. They seem to know those things that we emphasize well enough, but they do not have a grasp of the sweep of American history, and they are ignorant of many of its details. Perhaps we should consider how we might deal with this problem."

As a consequence of this discussion, the teachers eventually decide to make some modifications to their history program. They do not tell themselves that they are going to opt for coverage at the expense of African

American history. Nor do they tell themselves that they will emphasize increasing test scores. They tell themselves that African American history has to be contextualized and that students will only be able to fully understand African American history if they can connect it to some broad themes about American history. They will, henceforth, place more emphasis on creating this context. They are prepared to consider the results of their students on the state tests as a measure of whether they have succeeded.

Consider six things about this conversation:

1. *The conversation is evidence-driven, not just data-driven.* The teachers have taken into account a variety of types of evidence, including their judgments of how well students are doing based on their appraisal of student work. Some of these types of evidence are quantitative. Others are not. They flow from teachers' judgments of what they have observed in their school and their classrooms.

2. *The teachers have assessed the meaning of the test data in terms of their aspirations and goals for teaching history.* They have neither ignored the test data nor dismissed their relevance, but they have assessed meaning in terms of a framework they have developed.

3. *The teachers have a reflective conception of their purposes that is independent of test results.* They have not taken increasing test scores to exhaust the goals they have for teaching history. They view test results as one measure but not as the meaning of their success.

4. *The teachers view themselves as accountable in multiple ways.* They see themselves as accountable not only to the state for their test results, but also to the parents and to their own professional standards.

5. *The teachers have a conception of the importance of the legitimacy of their decisions.* They recall that parents contributed to the development of the program and are concerned that they keep faith with these parents.

6. *The teachers function collegially in a professional learning community.* They are able to make the kinds of judgments they make about their history program because they meet regularly to discuss their goals and learning strategies.

These teachers seem to me to be engaged in a process of deliberation and decision making that is likely to be effective and that has a strong ethical warrant. So far as effectiveness is concerned, the goals the teachers have are clear, and they have a reasonable idea of how they will recognize if they are being met. Their attitude toward decision making is experimental and collegial. They are prepared to change if the evidence suggests that they are not being successful. They discuss the meaning of the evidence with one another, and they adopt a collective vision of how to proceed.

Their decision making is ethical in a number of ways. It is reflective about ends and means. The ends sought are worthy ends. They are also legitimate ends. The teachers have taken the views of parents into account. They have upheld professional standards. They have placed the welfare of their students first. And they have been respectful of their state's testing and accountability program without letting it define the meaning of a good education for them.

DUE PROCESS AND ITS FRIENDS

You still have to decide what to do about Daniel Wilkins. Will you recommend him for tenure? Here I am not concerned with the substance of this question. Instead, I want to ask whether another set of standards for ethical decision making has been met. Due process concerns the reasonableness and the fairness of decisions. Questions of due process are likely to be especially important in personnel judgment and in matters of discipline. The idea of due process links the notions of fairness and reasonableness. Fair decisions are those that are made for relevant reasons and on the basis of adequate evidence. The rules and standards of due process are intended to ensure that decisions are made for relevant reasons and on the basis of adequate evidence (see Strike, 1990a).

I will not here discuss the legal requirements of due process, although you should know them. It is also important that you consider that what is fair may exceed what is legally required. This may especially be true in the case of tenure decisions for nontenured teachers. In what follows, I will suggest a number of ideas about what due process (and ethical decision-making more broadly) requires, illustrating most of them with the case of Daniel.

- Ethical decisions must be made for relevant reasons. A relevant reason is one that serves the legitimate goals of the organization. Schools exist for the benefit of students, particularly to educate them. Hence, making decisions for relevant reasons, in educational contexts, means that decisions are justified primarily in terms of their beneficial effects for students.

In the case of Daniel, there may be two problematic matters. First, Daniel is not a team player. He frequently dissents from the consensus, is "not with the program," and seems to go his own way, regardless of what has been decided. This is tricky, because an organization that wishes to be a learning organization needs to consider dissenting opinions and diverse points of view. That a person disagrees, even more than occasionally, should not be viewed as a relevant reason why that person should not be retained.

At the same time, Daniel does more than dissent. He is philosophically estranged from the purposes of the program and of the school to the point where he cannot cooperate with others to achieve common goals. Schools do have the right to consider the educational philosophy of the people they hire and retain and to select people who are able to cooperate with others in a coherent, collective effort.

Daniel also seems to feel free to ignore collectively taken decisions. He frequently does what he wishes, even if the group has decided on a different direction. That people should be able to express dissenting views does not justify ignoring decisions that have been legitimately made. Given what is meant by the claim that Daniel is "not with the program," these are relevant considerations in evaluating him for tenure. It is reasonable to believe that his alienation and independence have negative consequences for the education of the students at your school.

The second concern is that Daniel has a family that depends on his income and, if he were to lose his position at your school, he and his family would be significantly harmed. Do these facts count as relevant reasons? I have suggested that in the case of schools, *relevant* means relevant to the legitimate purposes of the school. Does this mean that the effect on Daniel's family is not a relevant consideration?

I am reluctant to draw this conclusion for two reasons. First, such matters may, at least indirectly, have an effect on the school program. That one is cared for by one's employer or that one is valued as a person, not just as someone who performs a task, may well have an effect on morale and performance. When an organization makes decisions solely on the basis of how people perform their assigned tasks, people may become insecure, a tense and hostile working environment may result, and performance may suffer. Many organizations have found that taking into consideration the "irrelevant" personal needs of their employees is not irrelevant to a successful organization after all.

Even if this is not true, I do not think that the effects of nonretention on Daniel's family can simply be ignored. Suppose that we knew that these effects would be catastrophic. Suppose, for example, that we knew that Daniel's daughter would have to drop out of college and that his elderly mother would be denied a necessary medical procedure and might die; would we still think these consequences to be irrelevant? The conclusion I would draw here is that we may take into account consequences of our decisions that go beyond our area of primary responsibility, but that we must regard these other consequences as having less weight than those consequences for which we are, in our professional roles, responsible.

Two additional thoughts: First, generally, when we set out to distinguish relevant and irrelevant reasons for decisions, the primary candidates for irrelevant reasons are such characteristics as race, religion, or ethnicity. When we insist that teachers be judged on relevant, not irrelevant, characteristics, we are saying that we should make our decisions based on the individual's performance, not on his or her race. The primary role of the distinction is to prevent discrimination, not to prevent humane decision making.

Second, we may take some comfort in the fact that we do not, in most cases, know the consequences of our decisions for the personal lives of employees. No doubt, Daniel does not wish to lose his job, but it may also be that he quickly will find another in a place to which he is better suited. Often when we worry about the effects of our decisions on the lives of those about whom they are made, we are considering short-term consequences rather than long-term effects, about which we are almost always ignorant.

Because these last two points lead to opposite conclusions, they may seem unhelpful. However, it is often the nature of ethical decision making that we must decide in the face of conjectural facts and conflicting principles. We must strike a reasonable balance. Striking a reasonable balance, nevertheless, requires that we be as clear as possible about what is at stake. But we should not expect that having clarity about our ethical principles will eliminate moral complexity or hard choices.

- Ethical decisions must be based on adequate evidence. Reasons for decisions must not only be relevant, they must be justified. Thus, there must be adequate evidence for these decisions. The nature of adequate evidence can, of course, be controversial. You have some achievement data scores for Daniel, but you also have reason to believe that these scores are not an adequate basis for making a decision. To take one obvious reason why this may be the case, these data do not tell you whether the students in Daniel's class are average, below average, or above average in their ability. Nor do these data tell you how much history these students knew prior to taking his class. Hence, they do not tell you the extent to which the scores of students in Daniel's class are a consequence of his teaching.

You also believe that Daniel is "not with the program." Your evidence for this is partly based on your own observations of his participation in teacher meetings, but some of it comes from the testimony of parents. They, presumably, formed their view from the testimony of their children or from observing the work their children were asked to do. Thus, your evidence about this is not systematically collected and is second- or third-hand. You should consider whether this affects its reliability.

You have other evidence. You have observed Daniel teach and, perhaps, you have copies of his lesson plans. But you are also concerned that these pieces of evidence are not representative of Daniel's actual teaching. He may be telling you and showing you what he thinks you want to see and hear.

It seems that the evidence you have with respect to Daniel's teaching is weak. What you may have reasonable confidence in is his behavior in meetings you attend. Is this enough to go on? Note that the answer to this question depends to some degree on where the burden of proof lies. A tenure decision is not a trial where the teacher is assumed to be entitled to tenure unless there is proof otherwise. One might hold that the burden of proof is on the teacher to demonstrate that he or she warrants tenure. If, however, you say this, then you should also believe that teachers are entitled to a fair chance to show their competence.

- Ethical decision making, especially about personnel matters, requires public standards and public procedures for collecting relevant and adequate evidence.

This is the core of due process. If you are going to make judgments based on relevant and reliable evidence, you must systematically collect this evidence. Hence, you need procedures for doing so. These procedures should be public. People, especially those who are to be judged, must know what they are. The standards that will be employed to make judgments must also be public. You must be able to answer such questions as, What are you looking for and why? What evidence will be collected? and How will it be judged?

There should be a procedure for "testing" evidence and the judgments based on it. In criminal trials, evidence is generally tested through an adversarial process. Witnesses, for example, must undergo cross-examination. This may also be the case in certain matters concerning teacher evaluation. Terminating a tenured teacher generally requires a high level of due process that may involve legal representation and cross-examination. This is not typically the case for tenure decisions, although there may be cases where evaluations are grievable and where teachers may be represented. Nevertheless, in most areas there should be a way to test the reliability of evidence. In many cases, testing evidence can be accomplished by an open process. In teacher evaluations, it is useful for teachers to receive a copy of your evaluation and to have the opportunity to respond.

- Decisions and the reasons for them should be public and transparent, consistent with the requirements of privacy and anonymity. You are a public servant, and your decisions affect the public welfare. The public has a right to know what your decisions are and why you made them. They are entitled to an opportunity to consider the evidence on which you made your decision and perhaps an opportunity to rebut it. Those whom the decision most directly affects have a similar right. Secrecy is the enemy of good decisions.

This principle must be balanced against privacy. The right to privacy includes the right of individuals to control information about themselves. Information can do harm. Generally, the reasons for personnel decisions are not made public unless the person about whom a decision is made consents. Moreover, experience has taught that there are benefits to anonymity where personnel matters are concerned. Letters of recommendation are more likely to be truthful when their content and the identity of their authors are not known to those about whom they are written.

We should recognize a cost here. When letters of recommendation are anonymous in this way, their content cannot be tested by those about whom they are written. Deliberations about personnel matters are generally conducted in private. This is the case both because this encourages openness and because it protects those whose case is being discussed. Here, too, there is a cost in accountability. Nevertheless, certain forms of privacy must be balanced against the general requirement that decisions and the deliberations that lead to them be transparent.

In the case of teacher evaluations, it seems reasonable that teachers whose contracts are not to be renewed are entitled at least to a statement that adequately explains the reasons for this decision. If you decided not to recommend Daniel for tenure, you have an obligation to tell him why.

- In personnel matters, those being evaluated are entitled to know, in a timely way, that their performance is unsatisfactory and to a reasonable opportunity to remediate their performance. One of the more troubling aspects of the case of Daniel Wilkins is that you have not told him that he is viewed as "not with the program," and you have not told him that this may be a factor in his tenure evaluation. Moreover, you have not told him, in part, because you are uncomfortable with judging someone because they frequently dissent.

Nevertheless, Daniel does have a right to know that the fact that he does not share the assumptions on which the program is based and that he does not follow it are relevant considerations, and he needs to be given a chance to change. This is a message that you should convey clearly and carefully.

- Ethical decision-makers avoid conflicts of interest. A conflict of interest exists when a decision you are involved in has actual or potential consequences that may benefit you or your family personally. As a rule, you should avoid participating in decisions from which you stand to benefit personally. When that is not possible, you should appropriately disclose your conflict. And you should be careful to avoid creating situations where you have conflicts of interest.

The case of Daniel Wilkins does not suggest any obvious conflict of interest for you. However, personnel matters can create such conflicts. Personal relationships are one source. It is difficult to be objective about someone you are attached to or someone you dislike. You should avoid developing overly close relationships with those you must evaluate. Here I do not mean that you may not like your subordinates or socialize with them. I mean that you should not date, marry, or become intimate with them. If they become your friends, your friendship should not go so far as to compromise your objectivity.

It is important to note that avoiding conflicts of interest concerns not only the objectivity of the decisions you make but also your reputation and that of your organization. You should not tell yourself that you are able to objectively evaluate people to whom you have become especially close. Even if this were true, it creates the impression of bias and that may damage your reputation and that of your organization. Avoiding conflicts of interest requires that you avoid the appearance of evil.

- The amount of due process should be proportionate to the importance of the issue. Due process has a cost in time, effort, and resources. We live in a litigious world where demands for due process can sometimes be excessive. The amount of due process required needs to take this into consideration.

The amount and nature of due process should be a function of two basic considerations. The first is what is required to have the kind of evidence that produces reliable judgments. The second is the consequences for others. Discipline provides useful examples. It would be impossible for a principal to fully investigate every charge brought against a student. Where infractions are trivial and penalties light, little due process is required. Students should have an opportunity to understand what they are accused of and an opportunity to respond, but detailed investigations into the charges and more extensive hearings are not warranted. It will generally be appropriate to take the word of a teacher without further investigation. For cases where more severe penalties are envisioned, more process is due.

In the case of Daniel Wilkins, what is most important is that there be a good program of teacher evaluation in place and that the decision made be based on the evidence this program produces. The Supreme Court has said that nontenured teachers whose contracts are not renewed are not entitled to due process under the U.S. Constitution because they are not being deprived of property. I do not mean to quarrel with the Supreme Court about the meaning of the Constitution; however, ethical behavior involves more than merely following the law. As a school leader, you are obligated to provide the best education you can for your students. This means that you need a good program of teacher evaluation. The requirements of creating and retaining good teachers should be the essential factors in determining the characteristics of this program. Moreover, while probationary teachers may not have a property interest in their positions, they are nevertheless harmed when they lose them. Humane school leaders will take this into account as well.

Remember that the point of due process is to design procedures and processes that ensure, as far as is possible and practical, good decisions. Good decisions are those made for relevant reasons and rooted in adequate evidence.

CONCLUSIONS

The discussion of evidence-based decision making and of due process can be summed up in the following way: It is your job as a school leader to institutionalize the rule of reason in your school. Decisions about educational programs should be made for good reasons, as should personnel decisions. In the former case, institutionalizing the rule of reason means creating a culture and decision-making institutions where ideas are put forward and discussed in the light of research and experience. This is the very center of the idea of creating a professional and collegial environment in your school. In the case of personnel issues and in matters of discipline, because fairness is a dominate concern, procedures for decision making should be codified. There must be public procedures for collecting and weighing evidence. This is the essence of due process.

7

Professional Community and the Ethics of Accountability

PROLOGUE

Why should we hold educators accountable? One answer to this question is that accountability programs provide educators with incentives to perform in a public system where otherwise there are few incentives for job performance. The success of an incentive system assumes that we can devise valid and reliable measures of all we wish to accomplish, and that we can devise incentives that adequately motivate educators to succeed on these measures while not providing incentives to behave in other, undesirable ways. I am doubtful that in education we can do either of these things adequately. If we fail, then we open up public education to three vices of accountability. I will call these *goal displacement*, *motivational displacement*, and *gaming*. Given that accountability is now a fact of life, we need an antidote for these ills. The antidote is professional community.

ACCOUNTABILITY AND ITS RATIONALES

Three Rationales

Accountability, as it is currently practiced in the United States, emphasizes the idea that schools should be accountable to the legislature for meeting certain benchmarks set by the government and, in most cases, measured by tests. *NCLB* includes the expectation that all children will be proficient in reading and mathematics by the year 2014. It also involves benchmarks concerning progress toward graduation. Right now, children must be tested every year from the third to the eighth grade. Schools are expected to meet AYP benchmarks toward this goal. Moreover, they must disaggregate test scores by race and SES (among other factors) and meet AYP targets for each group. Progress toward eliminating achievement gaps must also be shown.

Many states are also moving toward exit exams that students must pass for high school graduation. New York now requires students to pass five different Regents exams in core academic subjects. Schools whose students do poorly on such tests may be subject to sanctions or denied rewards. Sometimes funding is at issue. Under *NCLB*, persistently failing schools may have to pay to provide tutoring, have their students become eligible for transfer to a better school, or even face a kind of institutional death penalty—reconstitution.

Are such accountability policies a good idea? It is hard to tell, both because the results are not in and because people have not agreed on what results we want. Rising test scores are, other things being equal, a good thing, but we may still question whether tests measure something worthwhile, whether they measure it accurately, or whether we have traded something valuable, but not measured, for what we measure. Other things may not be equal.

And any educational reform should also be judged by its unintended consequences. We do not, for example, know much about the cost in achievement because of the amount of time spent taking tests, and we do not know much about whether there is a cost in alienation and disengagement for those who must take them and those who must give them.

Why would we expect this form of accountability to improve education? There are several story lines here. One story has to do with coherence. Schools will do better when curriculum, instruction, textbooks, teacher training, finance, and tests are aligned so as to work together and function in a mutually reinforcing way (see Fuhrman, 1993). This form of coherence requires clear content standards, which can be the core around which the components of the educational system align.

A second story concerns curricular equality. Standards for which educators are held accountable are key, some believe, to ensuring that the kind of curriculum offered to students in affluent suburbs is also offered to children in impoverished urban areas where, it is believed, expectations are often low and the curriculum often impoverished.

A third story (which has become the most important) concerns incentives (see Friedman, 1962). Here, the argument goes like this: In a market economy, there are built-in incentives for productivity. Producers must meet or beat their competition by providing better products and services at a cheaper price. If they do not, they will lose their customers to their competitors. The "invisible hand" of the market provides incentives for producers to meet the needs of consumers.

But education is a public monopoly. Educators do not need to compete for their students and their paychecks. Hence, they lack incentives for productivity. What accountability to the government for meeting test-measured benchmarks does is to provide these incentives. It does this via a set of rewards and sanctions that are contingent on test performance. These incentives include threats of lost resources and students. There is the significant threat of a kind of public shaming. After all, most states now have some form of school report card, where citizens can see how the students in their schools are doing and compare these results with other schools. If your school does not do well, local citizens and the district office may be on your case. Here I am concerned with how you will respond to this kind of accountability. Test-based accountability is most likely to succeed if educators employ its results sensibly. I also think it has certain potential vices. These vices have a cure that it is within your power to provide.

The vices I will discuss are three. The first vice is goal displacement. Educators will come to narrow their aspirations for students sometimes unconsciously or uncritically. Goal displacement has two forms. The first form is the narrowing of the range of aspirations. Perhaps a concern for citizenship or for the examined life is pushed aside. The second form is goal reduction. The meaning and depth of a subject is reduced to that which can be easily tested. The second vice is motivational displacement. Educators will cease to be internally motivated to do a good job and will rely largely on the incentives provided by accountability to motivate their behavior. They will care for nothing other than higher scores. The third vice is gaming. Educators will find ways to raise test scores other than by educating their students better. Many forms of gaming are harmful and unethical.

ACCOUNTABILITY AND PROFESSIONAL COMMUNITY

The cure for these vices is professional community. The basic idea is this: If educators are to be accountable, what they need to be accountable for is providing their students with a good education. How well students do on tests may be one measure of a good education, but it is not the full meaning of a good education. If this is correct, then educators have a duty to their students to have in mind a conception of the nature of a good education toward which they aim. They may then employ such data as they receive from the test scores of their students along with other evidence to make informed judgments as to how they can better serve their students.

This kind of reflection is a collective and collegial activity. It is valuable not only because it helps educators to know what to do to raise test scores.

It also helps them to create and maintain a worthy conception of what they are trying to achieve that goes beyond raising test scores. And it helps them to reinforce in one another the commitment to professional standards and to the welfare of those they teach. Professional community is the antidote to the vices of test-based accountability.

To make this case, let's begin with a review of some points I have made in this book. I have just mentioned one point: Test data should be viewed as one measure of a good education, not the meaning of it. There are two main reasons for this. One is that there are objectives that are important to a good education that are not likely to be easily measured by tests. These include leading an examined life, citizenship, and developing those capacities that enhance the enjoyment of life. Second, any test samples its domain. Standardized tests are developed under constraints of time and cost. They may often measure those features of a subject that are easiest to measure. They must be valid and reliable. These features constrain what they can and cannot adequately measure. Tests of reading and writing may measure reading comprehension or the ability to write a well-structured paragraph. They are less likely to measure the appreciation of literature or the ability to construct a sophisticated argument. Tests of science may measure content knowledge but are less likely to measure a grasp of how to employ scientific method, an appreciation of a rigorous argument, or awe at the beauty of nature. These facts about tests are not reasons to disavow them. They are reasons to understand their limits and to not have one's conception of a good education dominated by them.

I have also suggested several things about accountability. Any view of accountability must answer three questions: Who is accountable? For what are we accountable? and To whom are we accountable? I have suggested three answers to the second question. We are accountable for providing a good education. This should include human capital formation, an examined life, citizenship, and mastery of skills and capacities that contribute to human flourishing. We are also responsible for providing this education equally.

I have also suggested that educators should be accountable for the creation of several kinds of community. The classroom should be an intellectual community in which ideas are valued and discussed, a multicultural and democratic community where diverse cultures are understood and respected, and an egalitarian community with a sense that "we are all in this together." Furthermore, the teachers in the school should be a professional community in which professional standards are respected; where research, evidence, and experience are deliberated about; and where the welfare of children is prized. The school must be a deliberative community in which the views of parents, students, and community members are sought, valued, and considered.

There are also three answers to the "to whom" question. Educators are accountable to the legislature, accountable to professional standards and to the professional community, and responsible to the local community. It follows that when we consider accountability, we need a conception of it that includes, but goes beyond, being accountable to the legislature for raising test scores.

A final point we need to remember is that we have explored the tension between two strains in democratic theory. Representative democracy generates a conception of the school in which leaders and teachers are first and foremost employees of a legislature and have as their chief duty obedience to this legislature. It also generates a conception of the role of school leader as someone who is a conduit for legislative authority and a member of a bureaucracy. Democratic localism, on the other hand, seeks to create egalitarian deliberative communities in which decisions are reached via the discussions of equals and expresses the power of the better argument. These two conceptions of democracy, along with arguments for professionalism, generate tensions that the successful school leader must negotiate. The sovereignty of the legislature must be respected; however, within the bounds set by the sovereignty of the legislature, school leaders must create egalitarian professional and deliberative communities.

THREE VICES OF ACCOUNTABILITY

Two Stories

I turn now to the vices of accountability. Here I am thinking of the "standard view" of accountability, where educators are accountable to legislatures for raising test scores. To begin, consider two stories. Both of these stories are, in essence, true. I have changed details so as to not identify anyone. Moreover, my discussion of the views of a superintendent reflects conversations I have had with several individuals and, thus, reflects the view of no single person. I will present my first story as the view of a particular superintendent. Let me call her Jane Complier.

Ms. Complier was concerned about the difficulties her district was having in improving test scores on the state's tests. These tests were widely viewed as "good" in that they tested for higher cognitive skills and problem solving. Ms. Complier had two complaints. The first was that test results were unstable. Schools moved up and down from year to year for reasons hard to explain. Ms. Complier attributed this to the fact that some areas of the tests had to be scored by expert raters and, because the state had had difficulty in securing sufficient raters adequately trained, rater unreliability produced capricious scores.

The second complaint was that Ms. Complier had been unable to discover a strategy that resulted in significant improvement for her schools on these tests. She attributed this to the fact that the tests emphasized a high level of cognitive skills. To move forward on these skills would require, she thought, a significant reworking of the curriculum, investment in retraining teachers, and the development of teaching strategies with complex methods and speculative results. Doing this, Ms. Complier thought, would take time and money (neither of which she had in abundance), and she would have to invest this time and money on programs whose results were, at best, speculative. Ms. Complier wanted a new set of tests. They should be machine scoreable, and they should aim lower. Given such tests, Ms. Complier believed that she could move her district's schools forward by an approach that included some teaching to the test and test preparation.

The second story is not about schools, yet it suggests some important questions about the consequences of accountability.

Some years ago I had a colleague who regularly parked in a university lot without purchasing a parking permit. On one occasion, I observed him removing a ticket from his window and placing it on a small pile of tickets on his dashboard. I asked him why he didn't get a permit. His response was that he had done a rough comparison of the cost of buying a permit versus paying the tickets he accumulated. He had discovered that enforcement was lax, and he had worked out when campus police were most likely to check stickers and in which lots. He had also discovered that the university had no means to collect for tickets issued to faculty. The results of this cost-benefit analysis led him to conclude that he was better off not buying a parking permit.

These two stories illustrate what above I termed goal displacement, motivational displacement, and gaming. Consider the story of my scofflaw friend. Parking regulations and their associated fees serve certain common goods. They allow the university to regulate access to scarce parking in a fair way and, by paying for it with user fees, they allow the university to provide parking for faculty, staff, and students without inflicting an unfair financial burden on students, whose tuition would otherwise pay for it. They also help reduce the traffic on campus and make it more pedestrian-friendly while permitting those who purchase permits to actually find spaces. Parking fees and regulations were set by a committee that included faculty, staff, and students.

There are public goods involved in the parking policy: traffic reduction, fairness of access, fairness in allocating burdens, and respect for the decision-making process. My friend considered none of these public goods in his decision making. He considered only the personal costs and benefits. The university was not willing to rely on these public goods to motive compliance. They issued tickets. My friend, however, had figured out how to *game* the system. He was able to manage his parking so that the university's incentives were inadequate to produce the desired behavior.

How does this illustrate goal displacement? Essentially, my friend had no concern for the public goods served by the system of parking regulations. I do not know whether it had even occurred to him that there were such goods. His goal was only to park conveniently at the lowest cost.

This is not only a comment about his goals; it is also a comment about his motivation. A concern for the public goods associated with the parking regulations requires not only knowing what they are but caring about them. This, in turn, requires certain motives. One must be able to be motivated by the common good or the welfare of one's community. Something like altruism is required. One must be able to place the good of one's community before one's own narrow interest or to experience the good of one's community as one's own good. In this case, my friend was motivated only by his own needs and interests.

Here, goal displacement and motivational displacement are closely connected. My friend was, I believe, a good and decent person. He was able to take the good of the community into consideration in other matters. Indeed, he was able to take the good of the community into account in other parking-related matters. I doubt that he would have been willing to park in a life-safety zone were he able to do so and not be caught. He would be concerned for the potential consequences to others. I suspect that one reason he was not able to consider the common good in his parking behavior is that it never occurred to him that there were common goods at stake.

This example suggests two solutions to the problem of managing a parking system. One is to bring the incentives better into line with the underlying goals. The idea is to produce the desired behavior by making it harder to succeed in gaming the system. Indeed, this is what the university eventually did. It got a boot and a tow truck. It raised fines and figured out how to make faculty pay them. Second, the university might undertake a kind of program in "moral education" by attempting to explain the common goods involved and persuade people that they should act for the sake of these goods. This strategy relies on an internalized commitment to the purposes of the parking system; it relies on incentives and individual self-interest.

In the case of parking, I would bet on the boot and the tow truck. University parking systems are fairly simple. It is not too hard to "align" the incentives with the desired behavior so that we get the behavior we want and do not produce much gaming. The alternative is a kind of honor system, which runs on trust and a shared respect for common goods. In matters such as parking, an honor system may ask for more than I think we can expect of most people.

In the case of public education, we cannot abandon reliance on trust, a concern for the foundational aims of education, and a commitment to the welfare of students. Educational systems are complex, and it is hard to align incentives with desired behavior. Moreover, intrinsic motivation is important and often available. Educators generally want to do a good job. They care for their students. They value ideas.

Now consider the other story. Ms. Complier's reactions and her desire for tests on which her school district could succeed are quite understandable. If educators are to be held accountable, they need measures that are reliable, and they also need expectations on which they can succeed. At the same time, I was also struck by the fact that Ms. Complier did not have her own conception of a good education that she was willing to pursue because she valued good education independently of success on performance incentives. She was entirely motivated by the desire to raise test scores.

Here, too, what we see is a kind of goal displacement accompanied by motivational displacement, but its features differ from the previous example. Ms. Complier is happy to be held accountable for the success of the students in her district. She has made a simple appeal to fairness. "If I am to be held accountable," she argues, "fairness requires that I be held accountable for achieving goals on which I can succeed." About this she is correct. It is unfair to hold someone accountable for doing something if the measures of success are unreliable or if no one has any clear idea what to do to succeed.

At the same time, the changes Ms. Complier desired were based on a calculation of personal benefit. She might have said, "Well, there are problems with the tests and with devising strategies to succeed. But at the same time, the goals at which these tests aim reflect a praiseworthy conception of education; hence, my duty is to encourage my state to improve its scoring procedures, and I need to struggle to discover ways to succeed." But she did not.

There are two other factors we should consider about this case. Educational systems are complex, and basic educational goals are often vague and controversial. We might look at standards in this way. Content standards have to be justified by appealing to two different kinds of ideas. Let's use history as an example. To generate content standards for history, we have to have some conception of history—perhaps a view of its narrative structure. Should we tell the story of American history as one of establishing a prosperous and progressive democratic society on a largely unoccupied continent, or should we view it as a story of the conquest of an indigenous people and the establishment of a slave-based economy? Progress or oppression? If we do not have some narrative structure in mind, we will turn history into "one damned thing after another." Second, we need some view of why we should care about history at all. The history teachers in Chapter 6 had a plausible story about how history helped to create good citizens and a sense of community.

Once we have managed content standards that express a reasonable conception of the subject, we then face the problem of developing adequate measures of these content standards. Then we must align curriculum and instructional practices, and if we think that what we are doing in accountability systems is to provide incentives for success, we must also figure out how to align incentives so that the behavior we reward actually produces good education rather than gaming.

It is inevitable that a system of accountability that seeks to make educators accountable for students' success will have a considerable amount of slippage in all this alignment. Tests will be only imperfect measures of content standards, content standards will be imperfect expressions of an adequate conception of a subject area, and the conception of the subject will be an imperfect expression of our more fundamental goals. If this is true, then goal displacement becomes a real possibility and a real danger.

It becomes a possibility because attention will be focused on success on tests even though tests do not unfailingly measure content, tell us if students have a sensible conception of the field they are studying, or reveal whether they have become good and productive citizens. It is a danger because we may adopt educational strategies that pursue success on tests regardless of whether these strategies are plausible, given a deeper understanding of a good education.

I want now to turn to two examples of subtle mechanisms whereby the kind of accountability system we are putting in place might abet goal displacement and motivational displacement. First, I want to consider the very idea of standards and how accountability has affected the language we speak about them. Second, I want to consider how accountability might affect a sense of professionalism.

STANDARDS AND ACCOUNTABILITY

I'm sure everyone thinks that high standards are good things in some sense. But what exactly is a *standard*? Consider two potential meanings of the idea. I will call them *standards as benchmarks* and *standards as criteria of excellence*. These may not seem very different, but stay tuned.

Standards as Benchmarks

The standards-based accountability movement views standards as answers to the question, What do we want students to know and to be able to do? (It rarely asks, What do we want students to be or become?) Given this, a standard specifies something someone should know or something one can do. Typical examples: A student might know the multiplication tables or know how to find the square root of a number.

When we have created an adequate list of such standards, we have the makings of a curriculum. We can then create a test that is aligned with our content standards. When we have done this, we can make a judgment as to how many right answers constitute an adequate performance. When we have done this, we have created a benchmark.

If the benchmark is demanding, we can claim to have high standards. We can aggregate benchmarks so that we can have benchmarks for schools, school systems, and even states. Here, too, we have high standards when the passing score is high: 65 is higher than 55—hence better, more rigorous. This is what I mean by standards as benchmarks. Rigor and excellence are defined by these benchmarks.

Standards as Criteria of Excellence

Imagine that you have fallen into a conference of mathematicians. You have gone out in the evening with a couple of them to have a beer. They are talking about one of their peers, whom they claim is a first-rate mathematician. What do you imagine they would say? Here are some of the things I imagine: "Jones is an excellent mathematician. The new proof she demonstrated in her paper was highly original. She did more than prove the theorem she set out to prove, she did it in a way that was not only consistent and rigorous but was positively elegant. The way she reduced the number of steps in the proof from previous attempts was not only ingenious but generated new insights into the problem." Here the standards used to judge mathematics and mathematicians are originality, rigor of proof and argument, elegance, consistency, explanatory power, and insightfulness.

Or imagine a group of poets discussing a new poem. Listen again: "Smith's poem was inspired. It combined a beauty of language with a precision of phrasing and an economy of words. Every word was carefully chosen and exactly right. When I finished with it, I had achieved a new insight into the topic Smith wrote about." Here, elegance of form, consistency, beauty, economy of language, precision, and originality are the standards used to judge the excellence of individuals and their work.

I do not want you to respond to these examples by thinking that the difference between these two notions of standards has to do with the fact that the examples of standards as criteria of excellence are employed by university professors or others who are highly accomplished in their arts, and that this notion of standards is unsuitable for public schools. In my high school experience, I was blessed by having two excellent math teachers. In one case, my ninth-grade algebra teacher had us work through a proof that ended up demonstrating that $1 = 0$.

"Well," some of us thought, "we did not really expect this to make sense. Shall we memorize the proof for some future test?" No, that was not permitted. We had proved a contradiction. Math insists on consistency. We had to check the proof. After reviewing the proof, none of us could find a mistake. Our attention was called to a particular line. "Look what you have done here," we were told. "You've divided by zero." "Well, why not?" we thought, and we were off into a discussion of the mysteries of infinity. Here in the earlier days of elementary algebra we were introduced to the demands of mathematics for coherence and consistency, its resistance to the paradoxical, and its rejection of the contradictory. Often there was a kind of "gee, golly wiz" air about what we were discovering—perhaps the ninth-grade equivalents of elegance or awe.

Several points about standards as criteria of excellence:

- *Standards are employed to judge the excellence of performances.* However, in a way that has almost nothing to do with reaching benchmarks defined in terms of the percentage of right answers required. Standards here have to do with the rigor of argument or the beauty of language.

- *Standards are things to be internalized.* Someone who was able to recognize the validity of an argument but did not care if arguments were valid has not become a mathematician.
- *Standards can be recognized only by those with sufficient expertise.* However, they are difficult to assess in standardized tests.
- *Standards connect learning to belonging.* Standards are created, nurtured, and transmitted by the cooperative and collegial activities of communities, mathematicians, scientists, artists, athletes, and craft people. In a way, to learn to have high standards is to affiliate and identify with each of these communities.
- *Standards of this sort are transformative.* When people have internalized them, they are able to experience the world in new ways and what they value has changed. Just as people who have not learned the rules and standards of baseball cannot see a home run or a well-executed sacrifice, people who have not achieved some mastery of the standards of mathematics cannot recognize or appreciate an elegant proof. When we have learned not only to see but to value what we can see, our conceptions of what is worthwhile have been transformed.
- *The mastery of standards enhances the quality of experience.* We are not only enabled to see the world differently but to enjoy it in new ways. Much of what is worthwhile in life requires some mastery to experience.

This conception of standards is essential to any adequate conception of a good education.

Which meaning of *standards* is the right one? This is not a useful question. The point isn't to say that the advocates of standards-based education have gotten it all wrong or that we should reject benchmarks. It is rather to worry that the cooption of the term *standards* by the standards as benchmarks meaning will cause us to miss something educationally important.

What we are able to see or what we notice in the world is much affected by the language we bring to its discussion. If we think of standards as benchmarks, and if we attach the notions of rigor and excellence to the idea that standards are benchmarks, we will miss a great deal that is educationally important. The very vocabulary of accountability can be a mechanism of goal displacement.

Another example: I know of a large state university that has strong norms of faculty governance. Faculty decide the curriculum, who gets hired, and who gets tenure. At the same time, the administrative culture is quite hierarchical. Every administrator gets a letter every year with a list of objectives to accomplish. Provosts write them to deans, who write them to department chairs. There is not much consultation. When faculty come up for promotion, departmental faculty tend to judge aspiring peers by standards that I would characterize as criteria of excellence, but when folders leave the department, benchmarks became predominant. How many publications, how prestigious the journals, and how high the teaching evaluations are the questions asked. In this university, there are two cultures of accountability, each with its own meaning of standards. In this institution, department chairs find themselves negotiating between these cultures with different goals and different standards of excellence.

School leaders also must negotiate two such cultures. In a democratic society, the chief duty of leaders is to carry out the legislature's policies. Hierarchy and bureaucracy are inherent to representative democracy. Such discretion as agents of government have is delegated discretion and is likely to be withdrawn when agencies are seen as unsuccessful.

Legislatures are populated with laypeople who, if they are to exercise oversight, need benchmarks and measures for the success of the agencies they oversee. Legislators are not likely to show up in math classes to see if standards of excellence are expressed by teachers and internalized by students. They will want measures that do not require a grasp of various subjects, permit comparisons, and inform policy. The needs of elected representatives do much to explain why we think of accountability in terms of tests and benchmarks. These needs are entirely legitimate.

Contrast this with accountability to professional standards. The kind of accountability associated with maintaining professional standards is accountability to the norms and to the members of professional communities and, in schools, involves accountability for a type of teaching that faithfully and successfully represents a field to students. Some refer to this type of teaching as authentic teaching.

This is the kind of accountability that is involved when well-trained people evaluate one another's performance. In education, it requires a number of things. It requires a level of mastery of what one is teaching that enables the teacher to transmit the standards of a field to students. It requires the kind of understanding of subject matter that Shulman (1986) has characterized "pedagogical content knowledge." It also requires respect for and knowledge of research that is relevant to one's practice, along with the ability to appraise research, and it requires the capacity to function collegially in the kind of professional community that is now commonly referred to as a learning community. Finally, it requires the kind of language that employs standards as criteria of excellence.

What is central to professional communities is internalized norms. Professional accountability depends on professionals mastering and internalizing the norms of practice and of client welfare. Professional communities also require trust. They do not altogether require that every member of a profession be a model of virtue, but they do require that enough people have strongly internalized norms to permit the profession to engage in effective self-regulation.

So we have (at least) two possible pictures of accountability and two cultures of accountability that leaders must negotiate. One depends on benchmarks and external incentives. The other depends on internalized norms of performance, responsibility, and trust. What can we say of their relationship? One thing is that we cannot dispense with professional accountability in favor of benchmarks and incentives. Benchmarks are imperfect measures that we are succeeding in educating our students. They will not adequately capture the full meaning of a good education. They are unlikely to adequately capture standards of excellence.

It follows that we cannot fully rely on benchmarks and incentives to motivate teaching and learning. In the absence of an internalized commitment to a worthy conception of a good education, we can expect students and educators to respond to incentives with personal calculations of benefit and to seek to game the system. Because tests and incentives in complex systems are inevitably imperfect, we should expect that the use of incentives will produce some dysfunctional results.

The Limits of Incentives

There are other limits on an excessive reliance on benchmarks and incentives. Return to my scofflaw friend and the university's parking problem. The university solved its problem by designing more effective enforcement. It raised fines and figured out how to collect them. It got a boot and a tow truck. In doing so, it altered the incentives. Now when people calculate the personal costs and benefits of illegal parking, they tend to conclude that they should buy parking permits and park legally. The costs of not doing so are prohibitive. The university has defeated gaming by its design of incentives.

It is much harder to do this in complex systems. To do so, we need reliable benchmarks for compliance, and we need incentives that are tightly aligned to our benchmarks. If we fail to create reliable benchmarks, the incentives we provide will not fully be incentives for what we want. If we fail to have incentives that are fully aligned with our benchmarks, we will motivate behavior other than that which we want. When we work in systems where goals are complex, controversial, and subtle, our benchmarks will not be fully reliable. If we work in systems that are complex, incentives will not be fully aligned with benchmarks, and we will motivate behavior other than what we want. Schools have these characteristics.

Yet I doubt that we can fully rely on internalized professional norms, either. While I have some confidence that most teachers and school leaders wish to do a good job apart from external incentives, we are all aware of enough exceptions to this such that we should doubt the full adequacy of any conception of professionalism that relies exclusively on internalized norms and trust. Moreover, we should bear in mind that the legislature is responsible to ensure that public schools provide a good education, and, hence, the legislature needs evidence as to whether this is happening. This seems to suggest that we should have a system of accountability that relies on benchmarks and internalized norms.

Combining these conceptions is not easy. The imposition of external incentives tends to erode the commitment to internalized norms. Thomas

Sergiovanni (1992) tells this story: Once there was a school whose teachers generally arrived early and left late, often staying till 5 P.M. They were motivated by their desire to serve their students well, and they put in the time required to do their work well. Yet a few did not. They generally left the school as soon as they were able, often by 2:30 or 3:00. To deal with these slackers, the school created a rule: Teachers were required to stay until 3:30. Soon almost all of the teachers left at 3:30.

Motivation is learned. It is taught by institutional body language. When an institution's leaders and its practices convey a sense that people are trusted to do a good job, most people will respond by putting in the time and effort required to do a good job. When an institution emphasizes rules and compliance, people may respond with compliance, but their internal motivation will erode. When an institution's every action says "get those scores up or else," internal motivation will be difficult to maintain.

People who are dealt with on the assumption that their behavior is motivated largely by calculations of personal benefit will come to have their behavior determined largely by calculations of personal benefit. They will eventually fulfill the prophecy. Incentives easily create an alienated culture in which professionals are transformed into employees, feel unappreciated and disrespected, do only what is required, and care little for the outcomes schools aim to produce.

A culture of alienation may result from the experience of distrust. Standards-based accountability conveys a message of distrust. It is a variation on the theme "trust, but verify," which, of course, means, "We distrust, therefore we verify." It is human nature to resent being distrusted and to respond by saying, "If you will not respect my judgment and my integrity, then I will do what you require and nothing more."

Goal and motivational displacement may also be affected by our shared vocabulary. The two forms of accountability, accountability to professional standards and accountability to the legislature, have different conceptions of what a standard is. Criteria of excellence are different from benchmarks. I have not argued that they are inconsistent with them. The problem is rather that current accountability programs tend to tell us regularly what a standard is—it is a benchmark—and thereby threatens to rob us of the vocabulary to describe other kinds of standards. We will not notice the loss of something we lack the words to characterize.

Hence, the kind of accountability that relies on benchmarks and incentives has a tendency to alter the goals and motivation of educators away from working toward providing an internalized conception of a good education and toward aiming at benchmarks and responding to incentives. Internalized norms rooted in a deep understanding of subject matter, the foundational purposes of education, and the love of students are eroded, imperfect measures come to define success, and effort is motivated by calculations of self-interest.

GAMING

A good indication that goal and motivational displacement are taking place and the difficulty of getting incentives right in complex systems is gaming the system. What I mean by *gaming* is behavior that aims only at reaching a mandated benchmark and that fails to take into account the achievement of the underlying purposes of the activity.

The most obvious example of gaming is outright fraud—providing students the answers to the test, for example. There are many other examples: Teaching to the test with no consideration of the degree to which the test expresses an adequate conception of the subject matter is a form of gaming. Substituting test preparation and rote learning for inquiry and reflection is a form of gaming. Focusing resources on students who are "on the bubble" and ignoring those who are sure to pass or sure to fail is a form of gaming. Taking resources from areas of instruction not tested and placing them in areas where there is a test without consideration of student need is a form of gaming. Redefining the meaning of a passing score so as to achieve a politically acceptable pass rate is a form of gaming. Encouraging students to drop out or otherwise misclassifying them so that underperforming students do not take the tests on which the school is to be judged is a form of gaming. It is hard to say how common these forms of gaming are, but they seem common enough.

What is the cure for gaming? One solution is to view the problem as one of technical adjustments to the accountability system: better standards, better tests, and incentives that are better attuned to desired behaviors and thus less susceptible to gaming. We look for the educational equivalents of the boot and the tow truck.

No doubt there are things we should do here, but if we go too far down this road, we run the risk of producing a system of accountability that is experienced as coercive, disrespectful, and alienating by students, teachers, and leaders alike. Moreover, in a complex and varied educational system, getting incentive right without producing undesired side effects is most difficult. (To get a sense of this, one need merely listen to the current arguments about *NCLB*.)

The alternative is to consciously and conscientiously uphold the ideals of a professional culture and to transform schools into learning communities where the questions asked are about what constitutes a good education and how it is provided, where test scores are employed as only one form of evidence of success, and where professional norms are reinforced. If there is a solution to goal displacement, motivational displacement, and gaming, it is conscious, explicit, and deliberate attention to the values and practices that create professional cultures.

We need to have good professional reasons for what we do, reasons that are discussed and debated. And we need programs that are rooted in experience and research. If we engage in such program development, we may be able to view mandated accountability programs as reasonable checks on whether we are succeeding instead of allowing them to define our goals and practices. We may even find that success on tests is a bit like happiness. We are more likely to achieve it when we do not directly aim at it. This I know is easier said than done, but it seems to me to be one of the primary obligations of conscientious school leaders in an age of accountability.

The school leader must therefore find a way to balance different forms of accountability as well as different norms of legitimate authority. The school leader must be able to respect the sovereignty of the legislature and its need to monitor and motivate achievement through test-based accountability while also creating and maintaining strong professional cultures. It is a difficult role beset with conflicting norms and expectations. I am confident that capable and dedicated leaders are up to the challenge.

CONCLUSIONS

In the Preface, I informed (warned?) the reader that the value of this book would be to lend perspective, develop understanding, and pose issues rather than provide directives and recipes. So I am not going to conclude with any directives or recipes. I am rather going to conclude with some reminders of the basic lessons I have sought to convey about how to be an ethical leader of an ethical school.

The chief lesson is that you are first and foremost a creator of an educational community in which all members live well together and in which children learn how to live well together in the larger community.

Good School Communities

Some of the features of good educational communities are as follows:

- They are intellectual communities in which ideas are prized, discussed, and given provisional authority as tools of thought.
- They are democratic communities in which students enjoy equal opportunity. The weakest and neediest members of the community are cared for and receive the resources they need to achieve an appropriate level of capacity.
- They are multicultural communities characterized by a sense that we are all in this together while also respecting differences and individual rights.
- They are communities in which the success of each is valued by all because it contributes to the welfare of all.
- They are professional communities in which a praiseworthy conception of education is nurtured and discussed, in which teachers and leaders are colleagues motivated by professional standards

and the welfare of students, and in which a professional culture is encouraged and professional norms are reinforced.

- They are communities in which trust is present because all are motivated to create good schools where children learn and have a shared conception of what this means.
- They are communities in which trust is present because decisions are made collegially, fairly, and legitimately, as well as competently.
- They are a part of larger communities in which the views of parents and community members are solicited and heard, and in which their participation is valued.

Good Leaders of Good Communities

Who are you as a school leader, and what is your role beyond that of community builder? Here are several suggestions about who you are, and who you are not:

- You are the conduit for the authority of the legislature. Your role is to serve the legislature faithfully while creating a healthy educational community in the spaces where discretion is available and without allowing your school to become a mere bureaucracy where position counts for more than deliberation and power more than consensus.
- You are neither the tsar nor the visionary of your school. Authority is to be distributed and shared. Visions are to be collegially created, not imposed.
- You are not a mere administrator. You are responsible for the instructional program and for student learning, not just for the efficient operation of the school.
- You are an *elder*—someone whose leadership is rooted in a kind of moral authority extended to you because you exemplify the characteristics of an experienced and professional educator. You are task-oriented, fair, wise, and motivated by professional norms and the welfare of your students.
- You are the "first among equals," someone whose responsibility is to propose more than dispose, to keep people on task, to create the culture required for the school to succeed, and to initiate the larger community into the project of your school.
- You are the authority of last resort. I do not pretend that what I have just proposed is particularly easy or that you will never encounter recalcitrant people. You will, from time to time, need to pull rank, to coerce people who will otherwise harm the program of your school, and to make decisions on your own authority that many will resist and resent. This goes with the territory. You are more likely to succeed when this is necessary if you are trusted because you are seen as professional, collegial, and fair.

Good Leaders and Accountability

How should you be accountable?

- There are multiple forms of accountability. There is accountability to the legislature for meeting prescribed benchmarks, to professional norms, and to members of the community. Good leaders recognize all of these and find ways to make them work together to improve their schools.
- Good leaders encourage the members of their school community to approach accountability with a collegially achieved conception of a good education. Perhaps this conception will not be precisely what I argued for in Chapter 2. Nevertheless, a praiseworthy conception must involve a vision of the worth of subject matter (that keeps in mind the importance of standards of excellence as well as standards as benchmarks), a vision of citizenship, and a vision of human flourishing and how what is taught contributes to it. Educators are not accountable merely for discovering successful techniques to realize externally imposed goals. They are responsible to achieve a praiseworthy conception of the ends to which they direct their efforts.

We live in a complex and contentious age. It is an age in which visions of education are hotly debated in the public sphere, and it is an age in which power has tended to flow upwards into state legislature and courts and educational issues are more likely to be decided by politicians and judges than by educators.

This world has limited your discretion as a school leader. It has generated numerous mandates and benchmarks with which you must comply or strive to meet. Some of these are wise. Others are not. The danger of these mandates and benchmarks is that they will also create an alienated culture of mere compliance in which teachers and leaders are motivated more by incentives than by professional norms and in which attention will be focused on compliance and meeting benchmarks by any means possible.

If you accept the responsibility to create a school community in which people live well together while students learn how to live well, you must find ways to honor these mandates and benchmarks while serving a praiseworthy conception of education and creating a professional, democratic, and deliberative culture in your school.

Ethical school leaders serve the legislature while resisting the spirit of the age. They find ways to meet benchmarks while also honoring a higher standard of a good education. They create community in a world that wants hierarchy.

These are not easy tasks. They are the ones you must accept to become an ethical leader.

References

Abington School District v. Schempp, 374 U.S. 203 (1963).

Apple, M., & Beane, J. (Eds.). (1995). *Democratic schools*. Alexandria, VA: ASCD.

Ayer, A. J. (1946). *Language, truth and logic*. New York: Dover.

Baier, A. (1995). *Moral prejudices*. Cambridge, MA: Harvard University Press.

Bartlett, J. (1955). *Bartlett's familiar quotations*. Boston: Little, Brown.

Bentham, J., & Mill, J. S. (1961). *The utilitarians*. Garden City, NY: Doubleday.

Board of Education of Oklahoma City v. Dowell, 498 U.S. 237 (1991).

Bok, S. (1999). *Lying: Moral life in public and private life*. New York: Vintage Books.

Brighouse, H. (2000). *School choice and social justice*. Oxford, UK: Oxford University Press.

Brown v. Board of Education, 347 U.S. 483 (1954).

Bryk, A. S., Sebring, P. B., Kerbow, D., Rollow, S., & Easton, J. Q. (1998). *Charting Chicago school reform*. Boulder, CO: Westview.

Callan, E. (1997). *Creating citizens: Political education and liberal democracy*. Oxford, UK: Oxford University Press.

Chubb, J. E., & Moe, T. M. (1990). *Politics, markets, and the American school*. Washington, DC: The Brookings Institution.

Coleman, J. (1968). The concept of equal opportunity. *Harvard Educational Review, 38*, 7–22.

Coleman, J. S., & Hoffer, T. (1987). *Public and private schools: The impact of communities*. New York: Basic Books.

Descartes, R. (1956). *Discourse on method*. New York: Liberal Arts Press.

Edmonds, R. (1979). Effective school for the urban poor. *Educational Leadership, 37*, 15–24.

Edwards v. Aguillard, 482 U.S. 578 (1987).

Friedman, M. (1962). *Capitalism and freedom*. Chicago: University of Chicago Press.

Fuhrman, S. H. (1993). The politics of coherence. In S. H. Fuhrman (Ed.), *Designing coherent educational policy* (pp. 1–34). San Francisco: Jossey-Bass.

Goals 2000. (1998). Retrieved February 2006 from http://www.ed.gov/pubs/G2KReforming/index.html

Gutmann, A. (1987). *Democratic education*. Princeton, NJ: Princeton University Press.

Habermas, J. (1984). *The theory of communicative action*. Boston: Beacon Press.

Kant, I. (1956). *Critique of practical reason*. New Ynork: Bobbs-Merrill.

Keyes v. School District No. 1, 189 U.S. 413 (1973).

Kittay, E. F. (1999). *Love's labor*. New York: Routledge.

Kuhn, T. (1970). *The structure of scientific revolutions*. Chicago: University of Chicago Press.

Locke, J. (1960). *Two treatises of government*. New York: Cambridge University Press.

Macedo, S. (1995, April). Liberal civic education and religious fundamentalism: The case of *God v. John Rawls*. *Ethics, 105*(3), 468–497.

MacIntyre, A. (1981). *After virtue*. Notre Dame, IN: University of Notre Dame Press.

Matzke, N. J. (2005). *Design on trial in Dover, Pennsylvania*. National Center for Science Education. Retrieved October 19, 2005, from www.ncseweb.org/resources/rnsce_content/vol/24/4838

Mill, J. S. (1859/1956). *On liberty*. New York: Bobbs-Merrill.

Mozart v. Hawkins County Public Schools, 647 F. Supp. 1194 (E.D. Tenn. 1986).

National Commission on Excellence in Education. (1983). *A nation at risk*. Washington, DC: U.S. Department of Education.

A New Compact for Learning. (1994). Albany: The University of the State of New York, The State Education Department.

New York State Board of Regents. (2005, January). *Earth science exam*. Retrieved April 21, 2005, from http://www.nysedregents.org/testing/scire/estestja05.pdf

No Child Left Behind. (2002). Retrieved February 2006 from http://www.ed.gov/nclb/landing.jhtml

Nussbaum, M. (1990). Aristotelian social democracy. In R. B. Douglass, G. M. Mara, & H. S. Richardson (Eds.), *Liberalism and the good* (pp. 203–252). New York: Routledge.

Nussbaum, M. (1997). *Cultivating humanity: A classical defense of reform in liberal education*. Cambridge, MA: Harvard University Press.

Pierce v. Society of Sisters of the Holy Name of Jesus and Mary, 268 U.S. 510, 45 S.Ct. 571 (1925).

Plato. (1928a). The apology. In B. Jowett (Ed.), *The works of Plato* (Vol. 4). New York: Tudor.

Plato. (1928b). Euthyphro. In B. Jowett (Ed.), *The works of Plato* (Vol. 4). New York: Tudor.

Plato. (1962). *The republic of Plato* (F. M. Cornford, Trans.). New York: Oxford University Press.

Plessy v. Ferguson, 163 U.S. 537 (1896).

Rawls, J. (1971). *A theory of justice*. Cambridge, MA: Harvard University Press.

Rothstein, R. (2004). *Class and schools: Using social, economic, and educational reform to close the black-white achievement gap*. New York: Teachers College Press.

San Antonio Independent School District v. Rodriguez, 411 U.S. 1 (1973).

Sergiovanni, T. (1992). *Moral leadership*. San Francisco: Jossey-Bass.

Shulman, L. (1986). Those who understand: Knowledge growth in teaching. *Educational Researcher, 15*(2), 4–14.

Smart, J. J. C., & Williams, B. (1973). *Utilitarianism for and against*. Cambridge, UK: Cambridge University Press.

Strike, K. A. (1981a). *Liberty and learning*. Oxford, UK: M. Robertson.

Strike, K. (1981b). Toward a moral theory of desegregation. In J. Soltis (Ed.), *Philosophy and education: Eightieth yearbook of the National Society for the Study of Education* (pp. 213–235). Chicago: University of Chicago Press.

Strike, K. A. (1988). The ethics of resource allocation. In D. H. Monk & J. Underwood (Eds.), *Microlevel school finance* (pp. 143–180). Cambridge, MA: Ballinger.

Strike, K. A. (1990a). *The ethics of educational evaluation: The new handbook of teacher evaluation: Assessing elementary and secondary school teachers*. Newbury Park, CA: Sage.

Strike, K. A. (1990b). Is teaching a profession: How would we know? *Journal of Personnel Evaluation in Education, 4*, 91–117.

Taylor, C. (1994). The politics of recognition. In A. Gutman (Ed.), *Multiculturalism: Examining the politics of recognition*. Princeton, NJ: Princeton University Press.

Tinker v. Des Moines Independent School District, 393 U.S. 503 (1969).

West Virginia State Board of Education v. Barnette, 319 U.S. 624 (1943).

Westheimer, J. (1998). *Among schoolteachers: Community, individuality, and ideology in teachers' work*. New York: Teachers College Press.

Wisconsin v. Yoder, 406 U.S. 205 (1972).

Index

**CORWIN
PRESS**

The Corwin Press logo—a raven striding across an open book—represents the union of courage and learning. Corwin Press is committed to improving education for all learners by publishing books and other professional development resources for those serving the field of PreK–12 education. By providing practical, hands-on materials, Corwin Press continues to carry out the promise of its motto: **"Helping Educators Do Their Work Better."**

AASA, founded in 1865, is the professional organization for over 13,000 educational leaders across America and in many other countries. AASA's mission is to support and develop effective school system leaders who are dedicated to the highest quality public education for all children.